Queen Victoria

Queen Victoria

Scenes and Incidents of Her Life and Reign

G. A. Henty

Racehorse Publishing

First published by Blackie & Son, London in 1901

First Skyhorse Publishing Edition 2017

Skyhorse Publishing books may be purchased in bulk at special
discounts for sales promotion, corporate gifts, fund-raising, or
educational purposes. Special editions can also be created to
specifications. For details, contact the Special Sales Department,
Skyhorse Publishing, 307 West 36th Street, 11th Floor, New York, NY
10018 or info@skyhorsepublishing.com.

Skyhorse® and Skyhorse Publishing® are registered trademarks of
Skyhorse Publishing, Inc.®, a Delaware corporation.

Visit our website at www.skyhorsepublishing.com.

10 9 8 7 6 5 4 3 2 1

Library of Congress Cataloging-in-Publication
Data is available on file.

Cover photographs: iStockphoto

Print ISBN: 978-1-5107-2411-2
Ebook ISBN: 978-1-5107-2414-3

Printed in the United States of America

CONTENTS

CONTENTS

CHAP. Page
XXI. THE ASHANTI EXPEDITION, - - - - 160

XXII. THE AFGHAN WAR, - - - - - - 167

XXIII. THE AFGHAN WAR No. II., - - - - 178

XXIV. THE ZULU WAR, - - - - - - 189

XXV. THE WAR IN THE TRANSVAAL, - - - - 197

XXVI. THE WAR IN EGYPT, - - - - - 202

XXVII. THE WAR IN THE SOUDAN, - - - - 210

XXVIII. THE NILE EXPEDITION, - - - - - 218

XXIX. THE QUEEN AND HER SUBJECTS, - - - 229

XXX. EGYPTIAN AFFAIRS, - - - - - - 233

XXXI. BRITON AND BOER, - - - - - - 239

XXXII. THE FAR EAST, - - - - - - 250

XXXIII. THE DEATH OF THE QUEEN, - - - - 256

PREFACE

To give even an outline of all the events and all
the wonderful progress made during the long reign of
Queen Victoria would require many volumes, and in
the limits of one small book it is possible to glance
only at its principal events. Comparatively little can
be said of the life of the Queen as a woman, and
yet it is as a woman rather than as a Queen that
her influence has been most influential over the people
she ruled. Her domestic virtues, the purity of her life,
her example as a wife and a mother, her sympathy with
her people on all occasions of distress and suffering
have given her a place in their hearts such as no
monarch ever before possessed; and her death has been
mourned, not only as that of a Queen, but of a woman
privately and personally most dear to us all. Her
virtues have gained for her the admiration and respect
of people of all nations, and the outburst of sorrow
universally exhibited upon the news of her death is a
far higher recognition of her worth than any written
tribute can be.

G. A. HENTY

January 24, 1901.

QUEEN VICTORIA

Chapter I.—THE QUEEN'S INFANCY.

1. TO-DAY AND SIXTY YEARS AGO.

As long as time lasts it is probable that the reign of Queen Victoria will stand out as the period during which mankind made the greatest advances. Indeed, it is scarcely too much to say that the amount of progress achieved in the last fifty years is equal to all that was accomplished during the thousand years which preceded them.

When Victoria was born (1819) people regarded ten miles an hour as a rapid rate of travelling. Steam was still in its infancy, and although steam-boats were used for river and coast traffic, they were supposed to be incapable of performing long voyages. The telegraph was unthought of, and had anyone predicted that ere long a message could be sent to the antipodes and an answer returned in the course of a few hours he would have been regarded as a lunatic.

The art of photography was undiscovered, and people were not able, as now, to enjoy views of scenery of distant countries, engraved by nature herself, or to obtain for a trifle the likenesses of those dear to them. The weapons with which the troops of our own and other countries were armed were little superior in range or accuracy to the bows and arrows of the ancient Assyrians. The great mass of the people were ignorant of the art of reading and writing; communication by letter was slow and expensive; newspapers were scarce, and read but by a comparatively small number; the price of books placed them beyond the reach of the majority. The science of health was in its infancy.

Those accustomed only to the present state of things find it difficult, indeed, to understand how vast have been the changes effected, how great the progress made by mankind during the sixty years of the reign of Queen Victoria. To those born within the last fifteen years or so it seems natural to be conveyed at the rate of forty miles an hour to visit friends in the country, to send a telegram to distant parts and receive an answer shortly afterwards, or to converse with people miles away by means of the telephone. To possess photographs with the living features of relatives and friends, to purchase books and newspapers at prices which would have seemed marvellous to our forefathers, are a part of everyday life to the present generation. To know that our ships of war are sheathed in massive armour, and carry guns capable of hurling huge masses of iron a distance of five or six miles, seems the most ordinary thing in the world.

Nor in small matters has the change been less. The influence of art has made its way into the humblest households. Light and pretty papers cover the walls; the commonest crockery is tasteful in form and colour; and taste is shown in the production of the cheapest materials for dress as well as in the most expensive. However poor a home, it may yet be made tasteful and pleasing to the eye.

2. THE QUEEN'S PARENTAGE.

The Duke of Kent, the father of Queen Victoria, was the fourth son of King George the Third, and it might have been thought that a child of his would have but small chance of ascending the British throne. Yet so it was. His eldest brother, who became George the Fourth, married his cousin Princess Caroline of Brunswick. He had one daughter, Princess Charlotte of Wales, who was regarded by the nation as their future queen. In the year 1816 she married Prince Leopold of Saxe-Coburg, afterwards King of the Belgians, but died with her baby boy a year later. Frederic, Duke of York, the second brother, married Princess Frederica of Prussia, but had no children. William Henry, Duke of Clarence (afterwards William IV.), the third son, married Princess Adelaide of Saxe-Meiningen. They had two daughters, but the elder lived only a few hours, the younger but a few weeks. Thus it was that the child of the Duke of Kent, the fourth brother, came to be heiress to the crown of Britain.

Shortly after the death of the Princess Charlotte, the Duke of Kent married the widowed Princess of Leiningen, and she became the mother of the future queen. She was sister to King Leopold of Belgium, and had by her first husband a son, Prince Charles, and a daughter, Princess Feodore. The duchess, on her arrival in England, speedily won the hearts of all who came in contact with her; but her stay in England was then a short one, for she and the duke soon returned to Germany. The young Princess Victoria, however, was not born in Germany, but in England, her birth having taken place at Kensington Palace,

London, on the 24th of May, 1819.   Under ordinary circumstances a feeling of regret would have been felt that
the first child was not a son, but the hopes of the nation
had for so long a time been fixed upon the Princess
Charlotte that there was a universal feeling of satisfaction that a princess should again become the heiress to

Kensington Palace.

the crown.   At this time George the Third was still
alive, but was very old and not able to perform the duties
of king.   His eldest son, therefore, acted for him, having
the title of Prince Regent.

On the 24th of June the christening of the infant
princess took place at Kensington Palace.   The Prince
Regent was one of the godfathers, the Emperor Alexander
of Russia the other; the Queen of Wirtemberg, aunt to

the princess, and the Dowager-duchess of Saxe-Coburg were the godmothers. Dr. Manners Sutton, Archbishop of Canterbury, baptized the infant, who received the names of Alexandrina Victoria. In August the princess was vaccinated, being the first member of the Royal family who underwent that operation.

3. DEATH OF THE DUKE OF KENT.

From the first the Duchess of Kent devoted herself to the care of her infant daughter, and passed a considerable portion of her time in the nursery. During the autumn of 1819 the duke and she took but little part in public life, living quietly and happily at Kensington Palace, and walking every day in its gardens with the nurse carrying the baby.

Towards the close of the year the duke and duchess, with the Princess Feodore and the infant princess, went down to Sidmouth, in Devonshire, to spend the winter there.

A few days after their arrival the princess had a narrow escape. An idle boy, shooting at small birds, approached so near the house that a shot broke the window of the nursery, and passed close to the head of the princess. Naturally much alarm was caused, and a search being made, the boy was captured and brought in; but on the duke finding that the matter had arisen simply from carelessness he forgave him.

The Duke of Kent was passionately fond of his baby, and strangely enough this fondness was to some degree the cause of his death. Having taken a long walk on a fine morning in January after a heavy rain, he returned home with his feet completely wet; and, instead of changing his boots and stockings at once, he remained for a long time nursing and playing with the child. The result was a severe cold, followed by inflammation of the chest. Doctors were then summoned from London, but their efforts were unavailing. The disease rapidly increased, and the duke died on the 23d of January, 1820, within a fortnight of the first attack.

4. A MOTHER'S CARE.

The death of the Duke of Kent was followed a week later by that of his father George III., who died on the day that the Duchess of Kent and her two daughters arrived from Sidmouth at Kensington Palace. The Duke of York paid them a visit as soon as he heard that they had reached the palace. At his request his little niece was brought into the room. The likeness between the two brothers was striking, and the child stretched out its arms to him, and in her baby way cried "Papa!" The duke was greatly affected, and taking her in his arms promised to be indeed a father to her. His promise, so far as he could, he faithfully observed. He paid very frequent visits to Kensington, and watched with a father's care over the growth and early education of the little princess.

The duchess had been, by her husband's will, left sole guardian of the child, and nothing could exceed the loving care with which she devoted her life to her welfare. She was her daughter's constant companion, she directed her studies, took part in her amusements, tenderly directed the bent of her mind, and formed her character. That the princess's natural intelligence was of an exceptional kind there can be no doubt. Her memory was remarkable, and she mastered her tasks with an ease and rapidity which surprised her instructors. She was generally taken out daily in Kensington Gardens in a little carriage, which was often drawn by the Princess Feodore, while two ladies in attendance walked by the side. She seemed pleased with the attention that she attracted, and nodded to the strangers who drew aside by the path to allow the carriage to pass.

The duchess from the first encouraged her being taken out thus in public, in order that she might become accustomed to be noticed and gazed at. She was at this period a beautiful child, bearing a very strong resemblance to her father, and indeed to the royal family generally. Her eyes were large and blue, her complexion extremely fair, her lips generally parted in a smile. Her uncle, Prince Leopold, generously undertook the entire cost of the maintenance and education of his little niece. For some years he largely contributed to the expenses of the establishment at Kensington Palace, and of the visits which, for the sake of the health of her child, the duchess frequently paid to the seaside.

CHAPTER II.—CHILDHOOD.

1. A SIMPLE LIFE.

The danger which the baby princess had so narrowly escaped from the careless shot of the boy at Sidmouth was not the only one to which she was exposed in her early childhood. One day, when being drawn in her little carriage by a pony, a large dog ran between the pony's legs, and caused it to rear up and upset the carriage. The child might have been killed had not a soldier, who happened to be walking close by, sprung forward as he saw the carriage overturning, and swung her out of the way before the vehicle touched the ground.

As she grew a little older the princess exchanged the little carriage for a donkey, on which she rode every day in Kensington Gardens. Nothing could have been more simple and regular than the life which the child led. At eight o'clock in the morning she breakfasted on bread and milk and fruit, placed on a little table by her mother's side. After breakfast she went for an hour's walk or ride. From ten to twelve her mother gave her lessons; afterwards she would play with her toys, under the charge of her nurse Mrs. Brock, to whom she was much attached.

At two o'clock, when the duchess took her luncheon, the princess took her dinner, always a plain one; and after this had lessons till four o'clock, when she went out for a drive with her mother. On her return she rode or walked in the gardens, having her supper of bread and milk when her mother took her dinner. When she had finished, she went out and played with her nurse, and came in again to dessert, and at nine o'clock retired to her little bed, which stood by the side of that of her mother. Soon after she reached the age of four, it was thought right that a regular tutor should be provided for her, and the Rev. George Davys was appointed to that post, which he retained until her accession to the throne.

Several summers were spent alternately at Ramsgate and Tunbridge Wells, and at both places she was very popular among the inhabitants. She used to play on the sands at Ramsgate, where her mother permitted her to mix with other children, to build castles and paddle in the sea.

2. THE FIRST BALL.

The Princess Feodore having now reached the age of eighteen, her governess, Miss Lehzen, was appointed governess to the Princess Victoria, who had also tutors for the various branches of her education.

The first serious sorrow of the princess was the death of her uncle—the Duke of York—to whom she was greatly attached (1827). This was shortly followed by the marriage of her sister, the Princess Feodore, to the Prince of Hohenlohe-Langenburg. As the two sisters had always been together, and the Princess Victoria suffered from the usual drawback of her exalted rank in having no play-fellows of her own age, the loss of her sister's companionship was a serious one for her.

When she was ten years old, the princess witnessed, for the first time, the magnificence of court ceremony. This was at a juvenile ball given by the King to the Princess Victoria and the little Queen of Portugal, who was only a month her senior. Here the grand array of military in the court-yard, the picturesque uniforms of the yeomen of the guard, the purple and gold dresses of the pages, the magnificent hangings and decorations of the drawing-rooms and ball-rooms, the variety and beauty of the ladies' dresses, and the varied military and naval uniforms, must have formed a striking scene. It was generally agreed that among all the happy children assembled there, the bright face and unaffected manner of the princess rendered her one of the most charming figures.

3. A MOMENTOUS DISCOVERY.

It was not until she reached her eleventh year that the princess learned that she was in all probability destined to succeed to the crown of Britain. Hitherto her mother had most carefully concealed that fact from her, considering that she should not be excited by the thought of such a possibility, until her judgment was so formed that she would understand the heavy duties and responsibilities as well as the honour of this high position.

But it was now deemed right that she should know the truth. Accordingly a short time before the death of George IV., in reading English history with her governess, in the presence of her mother, she met with some point connected with the succession to the crown, which had no doubt been purposely introduced to excite her curiosity. After studying the question for some time, she looked up and asked her governess suddenly:

"In the event of the death of my uncle the King, who will be the heir presumptive to the throne?"

"The Duke of Clarence will succeed on the death of the present king," her governess said.

"Yes, I know that," the princess replied; "but who will succeed him?"

After a moment's hesitation her governess answered:

"Princess, you have several uncles."

The colour rose to the cheek of the princess, and she said seriously:

"Yes, I have, but I see here that my papa was next in age to my uncle Clarence, and it does seem to me, from what I have just been reading, that when he and the present king are both dead, I shall become Queen of England."

Her governess looked at the duchess, who, after a short pause, told her that this was so, and then spoke to her of the grave cares and responsibility of such a position.

The Princess makes a Discovery.

The princess throughout the rest of the day was grave and thoughtful, showing that the prospect which now for the first time opened before her excited no childish joy or exultation, but that she was rather weighed down by

the thought of the lofty position she would be called upon
to occupy.

4. EDUCATION.

The young princess must, indeed, have been a diligent
scholar. She already spoke French, German, and Italian
fluently; had a fair knowledge of Latin, being able to
translate Virgil and Horace with ease; and had made a
considerable progress in mathematics. She had great
taste both for music and drawing, a list of acquirements
exceptional indeed in a girl of seventeen, much less in
one of eleven years old. As soon as King William
ascended the throne, he requested Parliament to make
arrangements for a regency, in case of his death before
the princess came of age. It was settled that the princess should attain her majority at the age of eighteen,
and that her mother should be regent should the king
die before she arrived at that age.

The nearer approach of the princess to the throne,
caused by the death of King George, and the knowledge
that she now had of the prospect before her, made no
difference in the simplicity of her life, or in her unaffected intercourse with all with whom she came in contact. Thus one day, when out walking near Malvern,
where she was staying with her mother for a change of
air, she was running on before her mother and governess,
accompanied by her little dog. Presently she overtook
a girl of her own age of the peasant class, neatly dressed,
and probably wishing to enter into conversation with her,
she said:

"My dog is very tired; will you carry him for me, if
you please?"

The good-natured child, ignorant of the exalted rank of the speaker, immediately took up the dog, and walked along for some time by the side of the princess, the girls chatting merrily together. At last she said:

"I am tired now, and can't carry your dog any longer."

"Tired!" the princess said—"impossible; why, you have only carried him a little way."

"Quite far enough," the girl said. "Besides, I am going to my aunt's; and if your dog must be carried, why can't you carry him yourself?"

"And who is your aunt?"

"Mrs. Johnson, the miller's wife."

"And where does she live?"

"In that pretty little white house which you see at the bottom of the hill."

As they were talking they stood still, which gave the Duchess of Kent and the governess time to come up to them.

"Oh, I should like to see your aunt," the princess said. "I will go with you, so let us run down the hill together."

"No, no, princess," the governess said, taking her hand. "You have talked long enough with that little girl, and now the duchess wishes you to walk with her."

At the word "princess" the other child blushed, frightened at the thought of the liberty she had taken in telling a princess to carry her dog herself; but she was kindly thanked by the duchess for her trouble, and received a present of half a crown. She curtsied her thanks, ran off to her aunt's, and told her of the adventure. The half-crown was afterwards framed and hung up as a memento of her meeting with the future Queen of England.

CHAPTER III.—THE QUEEN'S ACCESSION.

1. A NARROW ESCAPE.

During the next two or three years the princess visited many parts of England, and stayed for some weeks in Wales. She made a tour through the midland counties, paid a visit to Oxford, and after a short stay in

Three-decker Ship of the period.

the Isle of Wight sailed along the south coast in the *Emerald* yacht as far as Plymouth. As the yacht went up the harbour here the princess had another narrow escape of her life. In rounding the hulk *Active*, which lay immediately off the dockyard, the *Emerald*, not making sufficient allowance for the set of the tide, ran foul of the hulk. The shock was such that the mainmast of the *Emerald* was cracked in two places, and the sail, with its gaff, fell to the deck. The princess was at the moment standing almost immediately under it, when the master of the *Emerald*, perceiving her danger, sprang forward, caught her in his arms and carried her to a place of safety.

On her fifteenth birthday the poet-laureate, Southey, addressed a birthday ode to her, which began as follows:—

> "Victoria! royal and benign!
> A wreath of verse thy bard shall twine,
> And welcome, with that strain divine,
>   A poet's lay,
> This season, sacred to the Nine,
>   Thy Natal Day!
>
> "A merry month hath May been deemed
> Since first an English garden gleamed,
> Or England's fruitful bosom teemed
>   With hidden stores,
> Long ere the star of Brunswick beamed
>   On these glad shores!
>
> "When regal glory gems that brow
> So humbly meek and gentle now,
> May England's haughty foemen bow,
>   And England's children brave
> The glory of their name avow—
>   The lords of land and wave!"

In the year 1834 she was confirmed by the Archbishop of Canterbury, assisted by the Bishop of London, in the Chapel Royal, St. James's. The ceremony was a private one, the King and Queen and the members of the royal family alone being present.

2. THE MAJORITY OF THE PRINCESS.

In the month of May of the year 1836 an event happened which was destined greatly to influence the life of the princess. This was a visit to England by the Duke of Coburg with his two sons, the Princes Ernest and Albert. The party spent nearly four weeks at Kensington Palace. Prince Albert, who was cousin of the princess, was of about the same age, and it is probable that the feeling which was some years later to bring about their marriage first sprang up in the course of this visit.

On the 24th of May, 1837, the Princess Victoria reached her majority, being now eighteen years of age, and the inconveniences of a regency were thereby avoided. The occasion was celebrated with the greatest enthusiasm throughout the country. Public addresses came from all parts, and in every church the congregations met to offer up prayers for the long life and happiness of the future Queen of Britain.

The Princess Victoria was awoke by a serenade of vocal music, accompanied by wind-instruments, beneath her windows. At eight o'clock the church bells struck up a merry peal, and throughout the day hundreds of the nobility called. A court ball at St. James's Palace was held by order of the King, who was too unwell to be present himself, and the whole of London was decorated and illuminated. Among the many poetical effusions in honour of the occasion that by the poetess who wrote under the initials of L. E. L.[1] was the most remarkable. It began as follows:—

[1] Miss Letitia Elizabeth Landon.

"When has the day the loveliest of its hours?
It is the hour when morn breaks into day,
When dew-drops light the yet unfolded flowers,
And sunshine seems like hope upon its way!

"Then soars the lark amid the azure singing
A seraph's song, that is of heaven, not earth;
Then comes the wind, a fragrant wanderer, bringing
The breath of vales where violets have birth!

"Which of the seasons of the year is fairest?
That when the spring first blushes into bloom
There is the beauty, earliest and rarest,
When the world warms with colour and perfume!"

It concluded with the following stanzas:—

"God's blessing be upon thee, royal maiden!
And be thy throne heaven's altar here below,
With sweet thanksgivings, and with honours laden,
Of moral victories o'er want and woe!

"Glorious and happy be thy coming hours,
Young daughter of old England's royal line!
As in an angel's pathway spring up flowers,
So may a nation's blessing spring in thine!"

3. DEATH OF THE KING.

It had not been supposed that the indisposition which prevented the King from being present at the ball was of a serious character, but he rapidly became worse. His strength seemed to leave him, and the idea of taking him to Brighton for a change of air, which had at first been formed, was abandoned. Day by day the illness increased in spite of the efforts of the doctors.

On the 18th of June, 1837, all hope was given up by his medical attendants, but he nevertheless attended to the business placed before him, and his last official act was to sign a free pardon to a condemned criminal. The next morning he appeared slightly better, and was wheeled in his chair from the bed-room to the dressing-room. He joined in the prayers which the Archbishop of Canterbury offered up for him, but from that moment he sank rapidly, and died soon after two o'clock on the morning of the 20th.

Immediately after his death the Archbishop of Canterbury and the lord-chamberlain left Windsor in a post-chaise to inform the Princess Victoria. They arrived at Kensington at five o'clock in the morning. "They knocked and rang for a considerable time before they could arouse the porter of the gate. They were again kept waiting in the court-yard. After much delay the princess was aroused and informed of what had occurred. She did not keep the archbishop and lord-chamberlain waiting, but in a few minutes came into the room in a loose white night-gown and shawl, her night-cap thrown off, and her hair falling upon her shoulders, her feet in slippers, tears in her eyes, but perfectly collected and dignified." Her first words upon being informed of her new dignity were addressed to the archbishop:

"I ask your prayers on my behalf," she said; and the two old men and the young Queen knelt together, and asked God to give her strength and wisdom to worthily maintain the high dignity to which she had been called.

4. THE QUEEN'S COUNCIL.

One of the first acts of the young Queen was to sit down and write an affectionate letter of condolence to her widowed aunt. She directed it to "Her Majesty the Queen." On placing the letter in the hands of one of her household officers it was respectfully represented to her that Queen Adelaide was now the queen-dowager, and that the letter should be so addressed.

"No," she said, "I wish it to be sent as it is. I am quite aware of her Majesty's altered position, but I will not be the first to remind her of it."

At eleven o'clock in the day the privy-councillors, to the number of about a hundred, assembled in the grand saloon at Kensington Palace. The young Queen entered the apartment accompanied only by the Duke of Sussex. She seated herself at the head of the council board, and took the usual oaths respecting the government of the kingdom. She then in a clear voice read the following declaration:—

"The severe and afflicting loss which the nation has sustained by the death of his Majesty, my beloved uncle, has devolved upon me the duty of administering the government of this empire. This awful responsibility is imposed upon me so suddenly, and at so early a period of my life, that I should feel utterly oppressed by the burden, were I not sustained by the hope that Divine Providence, which has called me to this work, will give me strength for the performance of it, and that I shall find in the purity of my intentions, and in my zeal for the public welfare, that support and those resources which usually belong to a more mature age, and to longer experience.

"I place my firm reliance upon the wisdom of Parliament, and upon the loyalty and affection of my people. I esteem it also a peculiar advantage that I succeed to a

sovereign whose constant regard for the rights and liber-
ties of his subjects, and whose desire to promote the
amelioration of the laws and institutions of the country,
have rendered his name the object of general attachment
and veneration.

"Educated in England, under the tender and enlight-
ened care of a most affectionate mother, I have learned
from my infancy to respect and love the constitution of
my native country.

"It will be my unceasing study to maintain the re-
formed religion, as by law established, securing at the
same time to all the full enjoyment of religious liberty,
and I shall steadily protect the rights, and promote, to
the utmost of my power, the happiness and welfare of all
classes of my subjects."

The calmness and dignity of the young Queen excited
admiration and surprise among those who were present.
When in any doubt as to what was next to be done
she looked at Lord Melbourne, who was prime-minister,
for instructions.

In signing the state documents put before her the
Queen signed "Victoria" only, without the "Alexandrina." This altered all the arrangements, for in all
the printed forms of the oaths which had already been
prepared she was described as her Majesty, Alexandrina
Victoria. In taking this step her Majesty showed her
accustomed good sense and judgment, for the simple
name of Victoria was far more pleasant to her subjects
than the long and cumbrous name by which it had been
intended she should be officially known.

CHAPTER IV.—THE CORONATION.

1. THE PROCLAMATION.

On the 21st of June, the day following the death of the late king, her Majesty was publicly proclaimed in the metropolis Queen of the United Kingdom of Great Britain and Ireland, Defender of the Faith.

A great crowd of ladies and gentlemen, all dressed in mourning, filled every spot from which a view could be obtained, while crowds assembled along the line of road by which the Queen would come from Kensington to St. James's Palace. She was greeted with tremendous cheers as she drove along, but it was remarked that the expression of her face was that of anxiety and grief rather than the pleasurable excitement which might have been expected to animate a young girl on such an occasion. She was dressed in deep mourning.

Coronation Chair

On arriving at the palace she was received by the officers of state and the ministers. Precisely at ten o'clock the bands struck up the National Anthem, the guns in St. James's Park and those of the Tower thundered out a royal salute, and the Queen, led by the Marquis of Lansdowne, president of the council, appeared at the open window. She was received with cheers and clapping of hands, the ladies waving their handkerchiefs and the gentlemen their hats. Completely overcome by her affecting situation, in conjunction with the eventful occurrences of the preceding day, the Queen burst into tears as the shouts of loyalty were heard, and the tears continued to flow until she retired from the window.

The heralds then read the proclamation, and as the last words, "God save the Queen," were heard, the loud and enthusiastic cheering again broke forth. The following verses are a portion of a poem by Elizabeth Barrett Browning inspired by the occasion:—

VICTORIA'S TEARS.

" 'O maiden, heir of kings,
   A king has left his place;
The majesty of death has swept
   All others from his face,
And thou upon thy mother's breast
   No longer can lean down—
But take the glory for the rest,
And rule the land that loves thee best.
   The maiden wept;
   She wept to wear a crown!

" They decked the courtly halls—
   They reined her hundred steeds—
They shouted at her palace gate,
   ' A noble Queen succeeds ! '
Her name has stirred the mountain's steep,
   Her praise has filled the town;

And mourners God had stricken deep
Looked hearkening up, and did not weep!
   Alone she wept,
   Who wept to wear a crown!
"She saw no purples shine,
   For tears had dimmed her eyes;
She only knew her childhood's flowers
   Were happier pageantries.
And while the heralds played their part,
   The million shouts to drown—
'God save the Queen,' from hill to mart—
She heard through all her beating heart,
   And turned and wept;
   She wept to wear a crown!"

2. OLD FRIENDS REMEMBERED.

Between the period of her accession and that of the funeral of King William the Queen remained in strict retirement in Kensington Palace. But even at such a time as this she did not forget the humble friends to whom she and her mother had been such kind patronesses. An example of this was given in the case of the family of a soldier named Hillman, who was with the Duke of Kent at Gibraltar, and had behaved remarkably well. When the man left the service the duke placed him in a cottage near the palace of Kensington, and, a short time before his death, asked the duchess to look after the soldier and his family.

The duchess had faithfully carried out his wishes, and, as the princess grew up, had often taken her with her on her visits. Hillman died, leaving a son and daughter. Both were in bad health, the boy especially, and the princess frequently visited him until he died. At the time the Queen came to the throne the daughter was lying ill. When the clergyman called upon her as usual— two days after the Queen's accession—he found the child unusually bright and cheerful, and she drew forth from under her pillow a book of the Psalms.

"Look here," she said, "what the new Queen has sent me to-day by one of her ladies, with the message that, though now as Queen of England she had to leave Kensington, she did not forget me."

The book was marked with the dates of the days on which the Queen herself used to read the Psalms, and there was a marker in it worked by the princess's own hand. This thoughtfulness for her humble friend, at the moment when such great events were passing in her own life, is typical of the character of the Queen.

Similar kindness was shown by her towards a poor man who had for the last six or seven years swept the crossing opposite the avenue leading to Kensington Palace. The princess had always kindly noticed him, and rarely passed through the gates without throwing him some silver from the carriage window. He received a communication, on the day after that of the Queen's accession, informing him that her Majesty had ordered that in future an allowance of eight shillings a week should be regularly paid him.

3. THE FIRST DEATH-WARRANT.

On Saturday, the 8th of July, the funeral of the late king took place, and a few days later the Queen moved from Kensington to Buckingham Palace, which had only just been completed. State ceremonies now took place in rapid

succession; levees and drawing-rooms were held.   Scarce
a day passed that deputations with loyal addresses did
not wait upon the Queen; and she held grand investi-
tures of the Orders of the Bath and Garter.   The first
great ceremonial in which she took part was the proro-
gation of Parliament (17th July).   The crowd assembled

The First Death-warrant.

between Buckingham Palace and the Houses of Parliament was enormous, and the reception of the Queen
enthusiastic in the extreme.   The grace and dignity
with which she bore herself during the trying ceremony
excited the admiration of all.

One of the most painful duties of a sovereign is that
of signing the death-warrants of criminals condemned to
death.   The first of these was presented to the Queen

by the Duke of Wellington; the offence for which the man was condemned to die was desertion from the army. The young Queen read it and looked up earnestly at the duke:

"Have you nothing to say on behalf of this man?"

"Nothing, madam; he has deserted three times."

"Think again, my lord," the Queen urged.

Seeing the Queen's anxiety, the duke replied:

"He is certainly a very bad soldier, your Majesty, but, as there was somebody spoke as to his general conduct, he may be a good man for aught I know to the contrary."

"O, thank you for that a thousand times!" the Queen exclaimed, and, hastily writing "Pardoned" in large letters on the fatal paper, she gave it to the duke with a hand trembling with eagerness and emotion.

4. THE CEREMONY.

It was not until a year after the Queen had ascended the throne that her coronation took place, the 28th of June, 1838, being selected for the ceremony. The interest in the occasion was immense, and London was thronged with visitors from all parts of the country. At sunrise a royal salute was fired in St. James's Park, and the bells of all the churches at once broke out into merry chimes. Even thus early a number of persons gathered in the park, and the crowd steadily increased until the hour fixed for the ceremony. At this time the multitude assembled in the park, and along the route which would be followed, was enormous.

At four o'clock in the morning a continuous line of carriages poured down towards Westminster Abbey, the doors of which were thrown open at five o'clock, and the whole of the seats allotted to the public were instantly filled. Two ranges of galleries had been erected on each side of the centre aisle of the Abbey. A platform, reached by five steps, was formed at the intersection of the choir and transept, and on this a chair was placed on which the Queen was to sit to receive the homage of the peers. At eight o'clock the peers and peeresses, in their robes of state, began to enter; their coronets were borne by pages, the trains of the peeresses being also supported by pages.

By nine o'clock all those who had the privilege of assembling in the Abbey had reached their places. At ten minutes past ten the royal procession set out. It was headed by the carriages of the resident ministers from foreign countries, followed by those of the ambassadors sent over specially to take part in the ceremony. Then came the carriages of the members of the royal family, and then twelve royal carriages with the lords and ladies in attendance on the Queen; last of all was the state carriage with her Majesty. The procession wound its way to the great western entrance of Westminster Abbey amid loud cheering along the whole line of route. The Queen was manifestly greatly affected by the outburst of loyalty with which she was greeted. At the close of the long and imposing ceremony the royal procession returned to Buckingham Palace.

CHAPTER V.—THE QUEEN'S MARRIAGE.

1. A NERVOUS TASK.

The Queen had at her accession found the affairs of the country in the hands of a Whig ministry, at the head of which was Lord Melbourne, who naturally became the Queen's chief adviser. He was a nobleman of great kindness of heart and engaging manners, and he felt towards the young sovereign, to whom circumstances had placed him in the position approaching that of a guardian and adviser, an almost paternal affection, while she on her part gave him her whole confidence and esteem. No great measures were carried during the first two or three years of the Queen's reign.

In 1837 Mr. Rowland Hill published a pamphlet advocating the establishment of a general penny post. Previous to this time the cost of postage had varied according to the distance. A letter from one part of a town to another cost 2d.; one from Reading to London, 7d.; from Aberdeen, 1s. 3$\frac{1}{2}d$.; from Belfast, 1s. 4d. The proposal attracted great attention, and a great number of petitions were presented in favour of its being adopted. The post-office authorities opposed it, but it was carried in 1839.

The time was now coming when the Queen was no longer to stand alone. In October, 1839, the Princes Ernest and Albert of Coburg again visited England. The Queen's preference was evidently for the younger brother, and on the 15th of the month the engagement between them took place.

Queens are placed in a different position to other women. It is they who have to make the advances to those in a station beneath them, and the Queen was obliged to propose to Prince Albert. It must have been a nervous undertaking, and she herself felt it to be so, for sometime afterwards she saw the Duchess of Gloucester in London and told her that she was to make the declaration of her engagement to the council on the

following day.   The duchess remarked that it was a
nervous task.   "Yes," the Queen replied; "but I did a

The Queen, at the age of twenty-two.

much more nervous thing a few days ago when I had to
propose to Prince Albert."

The prince, writing of the event to his affectionate
grandmother, said:

"The Queen sent for me alone to her room the other day, and declared to me in a genuine outburst of affection that I have gained her whole heart, and would make her intensely happy if I would make her the sacrifice of sharing her life with her, for she said she looked upon it as a sacrifice. The only thing that troubled her was that she did not think she was worthy of me."

2. THE ANNOUNCEMENT OF THE ENGAGEMENT.

It would hardly be thought at first sight that there was any great sacrifice on the part of a small German prince in marrying the Queen of Britain; but there can be no doubt that in many respects it was a sacrifice, and a great one. The position of the husband of a queen is one of great difficulty. As a foreigner he is viewed with a certain amount of jealousy and even of dislike. Every action is criticised and misinterpreted. Much of his time has to be taken up with state ceremonials, and he loses all that freedom which is the right of a private individual without gaining the power and honour which belong to a king.

Prince Albert's private fortune though not large was amply sufficient for all his needs, and the income which came to him as Prince Consort could add nothing to his enjoyments. The prince was a man of unusual culture and talent. He painted well and was an excellent musician, being able to compose as well as to perform music. He was very well read and was a bright and pleasant companion, and took a great interest in literature and art. As his character became known and understood by the nation he won the affection of the English people, and at his death was deeply and generally lamented.

It was not until late in November, 1839, that the Queen went up to town from Windsor and held a council to inform her ministers of the important step she had taken. The following is the declaration in which she made known to them the fact:—

"I have caused you to be summoned at the present time in order that I may acquaint you with my resolution in a matter which deeply concerns the welfare of my people and the happiness of my future life. It is my intention to ally myself in marriage with the Prince Albert of Saxe-Coburg and Gotha.

Prince Albert.

Deeply impressed with the solemnity of the engagement which I am about to contract I have not come to this decision without mature consideration, nor without feeling a strong assurance that, with the blessing of Almighty God, it will at once secure my domestic felicity and serve the interests of my country. I have thought fit to make known this resolution to you at this early period in order that you may be apprised of a matter so highly important to me and to my kingdom, and which I persuade myself will be most acceptable to all my loving subjects."

At the opening of Parliament (16th January, 1840) the Queen made known her engagement. A bill was passed for making Prince Albert a British subject, and an annuity of thirty thousand a year was settled upon him. The prince arrived in England again on the 8th of February, and on the 10th the marriage was solemnized. It took place in St. James's. The ceremony was a very grand one, all the great personages of the kingdom being present.

3. A DASTARDLY ATTEMPT.

During the next few months the newly married couple spent part of their time quietly at Windsor. On the 10th of June when they were in London an event took place which caused a very painful sensation in the country. As the Queen and Prince Albert were driving up Constitution Hill a young man stepped forward, presented a pistol and fired at the Queen. A moment later he drew another pistol and, taking a very deliberate aim, fired again. Happily neither of the bullets took effect, and the fellow was at once seized by the indignant spectators. He was taken to the police station, and was found to be a youth named Edward Oxford, who had been employed as a barman at a public-house.

He was tried for the attempt on the Queen's life, and the jury found him guilty, but declared him to be out of his mind. He was kept for thirty-five years in a lunatic asylum, and as he showed no other signs of madness he was then released on his promise to emigrate at once to Australia.

The princess royal was born at Buckingham Palace on the 21st of November, 1840, and the event caused great rejoicing. Upon the day before that fixed for the christening of the infant princess an accident happened to Prince Albert which might have been very serious. He was skating on the piece of water in the gardens of Buckingham Palace when the ice suddenly broke and he fell in. The greatest consternation seized the ladies and others who happened to be present. But the Queen showed a wonderful calmness and presence of mind. She made her way along the ice to the edge of the hole and stretched out her hand to the prince and held him up until assistance arrived.

In 1841 Lord Melbourne's government was defeated, and Sir Robert Peel became prime-minister. The new government at once set themselves to grapple with the deficiency in the national finances, established the property and income tax, and took off a large number of petty and irritating taxes.

About this time there were brought forward in Parliament a great many measures which showed the increasing interest felt in the happiness and well-doing of the working-classes. Among them were factory bills, education bills, and bills designed to put an end to the over-working and ill-treatment of women and children in mines and factories. Outside Parliament the same feeling displayed itself in movements for the early closing of shops, for the erection of model lodging-houses, and in many other benevolent schemes.

The following are some of the verses by Mrs. Browning on the hardships suffered by children prior to the passing of the factory act:—

THE CRY OF THE CHILDREN.

Do ye hear the children weeping, O my brothers,
    Ere the sorrow comes with years?
They are leaning their young heads against their mothers,—
    And *that* cannot stop their tears.
The young lambs are bleating in the meadows,
   The young birds are chirping in the nest,
The young fawns are playing with the shadows,
   The young flowers are blowing toward the west—
But the young, young children, O my brothers,
    They are weeping bitterly!—
They are weeping in the playtime of the others,
    In the country of the free.

They look up with their pale and sunken faces,
    And their looks are sad to see,
For the man's hoary anguish draws and presses
    Down the cheeks of infancy—
"Your old earth," they say, "is very dreary;"
   "Our young feet," they say, "are very weak!
Few paces have we taken, yet are weary—
    Our grave-rest is very far to seek.
Ask the aged why they weep, and not the children,
    For the outside earth is cold,
And we young ones stand without, in our bewildering,
    And the graves are for the old.

"For oh," say the children, "we are weary,
    And we cannot run or leap—
If we cared for any meadows, it were merely
    To drop down in them and sleep.
Our knees tremble sorely in the stooping—
   We fall upon our faces, trying to go;

And, underneath our heavy eyelids drooping,
  The reddest flower would look as pale as snow.
For, all day, we drag our burden tiring
    Through the coal-dark underground—
Or, all day, we drive the wheels of iron
    In the factories, round and round.

" For, all day, the wheels are droning, turning,—
    Their wind comes in our faces,—
Till our hearts turn,—our head, with pulses burning,
    And the walls turn in their places—
Turns the sky in the high window blank and reeling—
  Turns the long light that drops adown the wall—
Turn the black flies that crawl along the ceiling—
  All are turning, all the day, and we with all.—
And all the day, the iron wheels are droning;
    And sometimes we could pray,
'O ye wheels,' (breaking out in a mad moaning),
    'Stop! be silent for to-day!'"

Ay! be silent! Let them hear each other breathing
    For a moment, mouth to mouth—
Let them touch each other's hands, in a fresh wreathing
    Of their tender human youth!
Let them feel that this cold metallic motion
  Is not all the life God fashions or reveals-
Let them prove their living souls against the notion
  That they live in you, or under you, O wheels!—
Still, all day, the iron wheels go onward,
    Grinding life down from its mark;
And the children's souls, which God is calling sunward,
    Spin on blindly in the dark.

4. BIRTH OF THE PRINCE OF WALES.

On the 9th of November, 1841, the Prince of Wales was born, to the great joy of the nation. The Queen herself, as a testimony of the joy she felt on this occasion, requested the home secretary to see that all convicts who had behaved well in prison should have their punishment lessened, and that those who had deserved pardon should at once be set at liberty. When the prince was a month old he was created Prince of Wales and Earl of Chester, and on the 25th of January was christened in St. George's Chapel, Windsor.

Twice during the year 1842 attempts were made to assassinate the Queen. The first was by a man named John Francis, and took place on the evening of the 30th of May as she was driving down Constitution Hill. He fired at the royal carriage when he was no more than seven feet away, but as in the case of Oxford the bullet missed.

The man had made a similar attempt on the previous Sunday, when, as the royal party were on their way to the Chapel Royal, Prince Albert saw him step out of the crowd and snap a pistol at him. It did not go off, and the man escaped. The Queen behaved on this occasion, as on that of Oxford's attempt, with the greatest calmness and presence of mind, and attended the royal Italian opera on the same evening to show herself to her subjects. She was received with the greatest enthusiasm. Francis was tried, found guilty, and sentenced to death, but the Queen granted him a reprieve and he was transported for life.

On the very day following that on which she granted

the reprieve to Francis another attempt on her life was made, and again as she was driving to church. This was made by a lad who levelled a pistol and attempted to fire it. Fortunately it did not go off. He was immediately seized and handed over to the police. As it was evident that all these attempts had been made not from any personal animosity against the Queen but simply from a desire for notoriety, a special law was passed making attempts on the Queen's life punishable by transportation for seven years or imprisonment for a period not exceeding three years; the culprit, moreover, was to be flogged.

Chapter VI.—TROUBLES ABROAD.

1. THE MASSACRE OF CABUL.

Very early in the reign of the Queen the country became engaged in hostilities in Asia. In 1838 a British army had entered Afghanistan to replace an Afghan prince, our ally, upon the throne, from which he had been driven by a rival. The task was achieved after some hard fighting, especially at the town of Ghuznee, which the Afghans believed to be impregnable. It was, however, carried by our troops after a few hours' fighting; at length all resistance ceased, and a strong British force remained for the protection of our ally at Cabul, his capital.

Towards the end of 1841 one of the greatest misfortunes which ever happened to British arms befell this force. On the 2d of November the inhabitants of Cabul rose in rebellion, and the tribesmen from all the country round flocked down. Supplies were cut off, and the

position became very serious.   Unfortunately General
Elphinstone, who was in command, was old, an invalid,

City of Cabul.

and wholly incapable of facing the dangers of the position.   Although he had four thousand five hundred

fighting men with him he decided upon retreating. The movement commenced on the 6th of January, 1842, and the force was encumbered by some twelve thousand camp-followers, besides women and children.

The cold was bitter, the snow lay deep on the ground, and the ravines through which they had to pass swarmed with an active enemy. The column was attacked on all sides. Numbed with cold, overpowered by fatigue, with the passage blocked by fallen animals and broken baggage carts, the soldiers fought to the last, but of the whole seventeen thousand persons who left Cabul one only, Dr. Brydon, reached Jellalabad in safety. All the rest had fallen, either from cold or the sword of the enemy, except a hundred and five, men, women, and children, taken prisoners by the Afghans.

2. THE DEFENCE OF JELLALABAD.

Sir Robert Sale was with a brigade on the way down from Cabul when the news overtook him of the rising in that town. He was at once attacked by the tribesmen, but fought his way down to Jellalabad, and determined to establish himself there. The prospect was a gloomy one. He was far away from succour or support; the walls of the town were in ruins, and in many places were not more than two feet high; their circumference, a mile and a quarter, was too great to be properly defended by so small a force. Nevertheless for months the little force maintained itself, sallying out and attacking the enemy whenever they approached, and driving in cattle. At last, after a five months' siege, the garrison boldly marched out, attacked the besieging army in their camp, completely routed them, and captured all their cannon.

Shortly afterwards General Pollock, with a relieving army, fought his way up the Khyber Pass and reached Jellalabad. The united force then moved forward towards Cabul, defeating the Afghans whenever they ventured to oppose them. On reaching Cabul the great bazaar there was burnt as a punishment to the town for the part the inhabitants had taken in the massacre, and the army then marched back to India.

While the fighting had been going on in Afghanistan England was engaged in a war further east. Disputes had arisen with the Chinese, who at that time regarded all Europeans with contempt, and behaved towards them with the greatest insolence, and paid little regard to any treaties they made with them. Accordingly, in 1841, our fleet sailed up the Canton River, silenced the batteries, and forced the governor to agree to terms. A few months afterwards the Chinese again broke their engagements, and the fleet, with a body of troops, attacked and captured several of their seaport towns without any formidable resistance, save at one town, where the Chinese fought desperately. As the fleet was advancing to the attack of the important city of Nankin, the Chinese agreed to all our demands. Many of the ports hitherto closed to us were after this open to trade, and although the Chinese were not as yet convinced of their inability to resist European arms, the first step was taken towards bringing that great country into contact with European civilization. From this step great results may arise in the future, for China is the most populous country in the world, and will probably some day play a very leading part in history.

3. THE FIRST SCINDE WAR.

In the commencement of the year 1843 war broke out between the English and the tribes of Scinde. This is a large province in the north-west of India, watered by the great river Indus, on whose banks stands the capital, Hyderabad. The country was ruled by a number of chiefs who held the title of ameers. They had been friendly with us since 1831, and the Indus was open to our merchant vessels, but, excited by the news of our disasters in Afghanistan, they began to plot with our enemies for our overthrow. General Sir Charles Napier was despatched with a small army to repress them.

Sir Charles advanced along the left bank of the Indus, several steamers accompanying him until he arrived within sixteen miles of Hyderabad, when he heard that 36,000 men, of whom 10,000 were cavalry, were in a strong position at Meeanee. Although his whole strength consisted but of 2600 men he did not hesitate to give battle, and on the 17th of February advanced against their position. They were posted on a high bank rising from the dry bed of a river. The position was about 1200 yards long, with dense woods on either flank, enabling them to sweep our ranks with their musketry fire as we advanced. Eighteen guns were placed in advance of the line. In front of the wood on our right was a wall having one opening half-way between the two armies; behind this wall was a large force of the enemy, who had prepared to rush out and fall upon our rear as we passed.

The general ordered a company of the 22d to hold the opening and prevent the enemy from sallying out. The little party did their work nobly; the opening was held, and the rear of the army was thus guarded from attack. The advance began, the troops pressed forward under a tremendous fire of the enemy, and the village of Kottrea was carried with the bayonet. The enemy allowed the 22d to come pretty close before firing, and then poured in a tremendous volley; but the 22d rushed on against their foe, who, armed with shield and sword, rushed to meet them, and a severe hand-to-hand fight took place.

Two of our Sepoy regiments came up and joined in the fight, and for a time the result was doubtful. Several times one or other regiment was driven a little back, but each time they rallied and pushed forward again, and for more than three hours this terrible fight continued. At last the British cavalry, 800 strong, came into action and charged down upon the enemy's right, dashing through his guns, and then fell upon the rear of the masses opposed to the British infantry. The enemy now began to retire, followed by the British pouring volley after volley into their masses, but disdaining to break into a run, although the British guns as well as musketry swept their ranks.

Even now, so disposed were they to renew the conflict and so great was their number, that the general recalled his cavalry and formed his troops into a great square, with the baggage in the centre, for the night. The enemy in this terrible struggle lost upwards of 6000 men—a number almost, if not quite, unparalleled in comparison with the number of the British. Hyderabad opened its gates the next day.

4. THE CONQUEST OF SCINDE.

But Scinde was not yet conquered. Shere Mahomed, or the Lion, one of the most powerful of the ameers, advanced against Hyderabad with a force even larger than that which had fought at Meeanee. When he approached Hyderabad the ameer sent in an envoy with the insolent offer: "Quit this land; and, provided you restore all you have taken, your life shall be spared." Just at that moment the evening gun fired.

"You heard that sound," the general said; "it is my answer to your chief. Go."

Four days after the battle of Meeanee some reinforcements reached the British. A skirmish took place before one of the columns could reach Hyderabad, the enemy attempting to arrest its passage. When it arrived the force numbered altogether 5000 men, of whom 1100 were cavalry with nineteen guns; and on the 24th the English marched out towards Dubba, where 26,000 of the enemy had taken up their position. This was admirably chosen; its flanks were covered by ravines and woods, its front by a ravine twenty feet wide and eight feet deep, with extremely steep banks.

The battle commenced at nine o'clock. A portion of the cavalry were told off to watch a thick wood to the right which was believed to be full of the enemy. The horse artillery pushed forward and took up positions where their fire took the enemy in flank. The first ravine was carried by the 22d, who marched up to within forty paces of it and then carried it with a rush. The fight now became hand to hand along the whole line, the enemy contesting every foot of the way with des-

perate valour.   At the village of Dubba, in which the
best fighting men of the enemy were stationed, the resistance was long and desperate, but the valour and
discipline of the British troops bore down all opposition.
The enemy were slaughtered by the terrible fire which
the artillery kept up upon them, and fell suddenly back,
pursued for several miles by our cavalry.

Eight hours after the battle had been concluded the
army was again on the march, and the next day the
cavalry arrived at Meerpoor, the capital of Shere Mahomed.   The chief had already left the town.   Terms
were then offered to the Lion if he would surrender;
but this he refused to do, and an irregular warfare continued for some time until all resistance was crushed out
by flying columns, after which Scinde was annexed to
British India.

Chapter VII.—UNEVENTFUL YEARS.

1. DOMESTIC LIFE.

In the autumn of 1842 the Queen had paid her first
visit to Scotland, a country where she was to spend so
much of her future life.   She received throughout her
tour the heartiest welcome from the Scottish people.
On the 25th of April, 1843, the Princess Alice was
born.   Prince Albert was now devoting much time to
the advancement of the fine arts in this country.   Under
his patronage a great exhibition of prize pictures for the
decoration of the new Houses of Parliament was held in
Westminster Hall, and many distinguished artists were
engaged in decorating a pavilion in Buckingham Palace

grounds. Mr. Ewing, one of the artists, writing of the simple life led by the royal family said:

"They have breakfasted, heard morning prayers with the household in the private chapel, and are out some distance from the palace talking to us in the summer-house before half-past nine o'clock, sometimes earlier. After the public duties of the day, and before dinner, they come out again, evidently delighted to get away from the bustle of the world to enjoy each other's company in the solitude of the garden. Here, too, the royal children are brought out by the nurses, and the whole arrangements seem like real domestic pleasure."

The princess royal was now growing up a very engaging little child, and a general favourite with those who came in contact with her. The Hon. Miss Liddell, who was in attendance on the Queen, tells the following story of her in a letter to a friend:—

"The Queen told us a funny anecdote of the little princess royal. While they were driving the other day the Queen called her, as she always does, "Missy." The princess took no notice the first time, but the next she looked up very indignantly and said, "I am not Missy: I am the Princess Royal."

On the 1st of September, 1843, the Queen started in her yacht from Falmouth for Eu, to pay a visit to the King of the French. On the way an amusing occurrence took place, which was told as follows by Miss Liddell:—

"I remained on deck a long time with her Majesty, and she taught me to plait paper for bonnets, which was a favourite occupation of the Queen's. Lady Canning and I had settled ourselves in a very sheltered place, protected by the paddle-box; and, remarking what a com-

fortable spot we had chosen, her Majesty sent for a
camp-stool and settled herself beside us, plaiting away
most composedly, when suddenly we observed a com-
motion amongst the sailors, little knots of men talking
together in a mysterious manner; first one officer came
up to them, then another, looking puzzled, and at last
Lord Adolphus Fitzclarence was called.

"The Queen, much puzzled, asked what was the matter,
and inquired whether we were going to have a mutiny
on board? Lord Adolphus laughed, but remarked that
he really did not know what would happen unless her
Majesty would be graciously pleased to remove her
seat.

"'Move my seat!' said the Queen; 'why should I?
What possible harm can I be doing here?'

"'Well, ma'am,' said Lord Adolphus, 'the fact is your
Majesty is unwittingly closing up the door of the place
where the grog-tubs are kept, and so the men cannot
have their grog.'"

At the landing the Queen was received by the King
and Queen of the French. They stopped at the Chateau
D'Eu, a place interesting to an English sovereign, as
here William the Conqueror was married. There was
a review of troops and several fêtes, and on the 7th the
Queen re-embarked for England, landing at Dover. A
few days after her return she crossed to Belgium and
paid a visit to several of the quaint old cities of that
country On one of the triumphal arches in a street of
Ghent was an inscription pointing out that the city had
been visited by Philippa of Hainault, Queen of England,
in 1343, exactly five centuries previously

2. IRELAND AND WALES.

In Ireland there had been for some years intense discontent, with the usual accompaniments of murders and
outrages, and in 1843 a new agitation for the repeal of the
Union had been set on foot by Mr. Daniel O'Connell and
had attained very formidable dimensions. The people
drilled and prepared for a rising, and at one of their
great meetings at Tara O'Connell promised them that in
a year they should have a parliament of their own. As
this could only be accomplished by force it was considered
an incitement to rebellion, and O'Connell and some of his
principal adherents were prosecuted for a conspiracy to
raise and excite disaffection among her Majesty's subjects.

After a trial lasting twenty-four days O'Connell was
found guilty and condemned to twelve months' imprisonment. An appeal was made to the House of Lords, and
the law lords found by a majority that the conviction was
illegal, and the judgment was reversed. But the trial
had had its effect; O'Connell had learnt prudence from
his condemnation and imprisonment, and henceforth was
far more moderate in his speeches. Other leaders, however, took his place, and the agitation in Ireland continued as before.

Riots had for some years been going on in Wales in
opposition to toll-bars. These had been erected on various roads, and the tolls greatly raised. No less than a
hundred and fifty of these toll-gates were attacked and
levelled by men dressed in women's clothes, who called
themselves Rebecca's Daughters, or Rebeccaites. Serious
riots took place, and the town of Carmarthen was attacked
by large bodies of rioters, who held possession of it for

several hours, but who were at last dislodged and dispersed by a troop of light dragoons. A considerable military force and a body of police from London were sent down, and order was again restored. As it was

Rebecca's Daughters, or Rebeccaites.

felt that the riots had their origin in real grievances, an act was passed altering the whole system under which turnpike-roads were managed.

3. THE FREE-TRADE AGITATION.

The tax or duty charged on foreign corn upon entering our ports had given rise to much discontent, as it made the price of bread higher than was necessary. During the year 1845 the movement in favour of abolishing this duty spread rapidly and became a great public agitation. The principal figure in it was Mr. Cobden, and he, with Mr. John Bright and several others, set on foot the association called the Anti-Corn-Law League. The head-quarters of this association were at Manchester, but it extended through all the manufacturing towns of the north. The bad seasons which had prevailed, the high price of corn, and the general distress combined to give strength to the movement, and it was naturally among the great towns that it had most adherents.

In the rural districts the idea of abolishing the duty on corn was viewed with the greatest alarm. The people considered that the free entry of corn from Russia and other countries would so greatly reduce the price as to ruin the farmers of England, and involve in their ruin the agricultural labourers and the dwellers in small towns whose well-being depended entirely upon the prosperity of agriculture. The question, therefore, assumed the nature of a struggle between the inhabitants of the towns and those of the country.

At first very few influential men were in favour of the scheme, and the supporters of the Anti-Corn-Law League were, without an exception, manufacturers, whose interest was entirely on the side of cheap food. The leaders of the movement threw themselves into it with immense energy. Meetings were held all over the country, and pamphlets and broadsheets sent out by the million. A bad harvest and the probability of a famine in Ireland, in consequence of the failure of the potato crop through disease, intensified matters. Sir Robert Peel saw the magnitude of the danger, and called a cabinet council in November, 1845, and proposed to them " that the duties on the import of foreign grain should be suspended for a limited period."

Only three of his colleagues were willing to agree to the proposal, but at the end of the month he won all of them to his opinion, with the exception of Lord Stanley, afterwards Lord Derby. But the great proportion of the Conservatives were wholly adverse to the change, and Sir Robert Peel, feeling that he had no chance of carrying his measure in the house, resigned. No other ministry could be formed, and he remained in office.

4. FAMINE IN IRELAND.

On the 14th of January, 1846, Parliament met, and Sir Robert Peel rose, and, amidst the silence of his own supporters and the cheers of the opposition, announced that his opinions in reference to the Corn Laws had undergone an entire change. Mr. Disraeli, then a young member, rose and made a tremendous attack upon his late leader, and was from that moment regarded as the head of the Protectionist party. For months a desperate conflict raged in the house, but a bill lowering the duty to four shillings a quarter was carried.

The increase of distress in Ireland was attended by a vast increase in crimes of violence, and government brought in a bill for the repression of crime. They were beaten by a large majority, and two days later Sir Robert Peel resigned office and Lord John Russell and the Whigs assumed power when Parliament reassembled on the 16th of July, 1846.

The state of Ireland had now become frightful, the potato crop had again failed, and starvation stared the greater part of the population in the face. The greatest efforts were made both by government and private individuals in this country to relieve their distress. Grain was shipped in great quantities to the Irish ports, but there was then no net-work of railways available for its distribution, and vast numbers of persons died. In the district of Skibereen 5000 persons died of starvation in three months, and a similar, although less terrible, state of things prevailed elsewhere.

At the beginning of 1847 measures on a large scale were brought forward in Parliament for the relief of Irish distress. The Corn Laws were entirely suspended, measures were adopted for the purpose of enabling the Irish to emigrate in large numbers to America, and no less than ten millions of money were borrowed to carry out the necessary measures for the relief of distress in Ireland.

While at home the attention of the nation had been concentrated on political events, a serious struggle was going on in India.

CHAPTER VIII.—THE SIKH WARS.

1. THE BATTLE OF MOODKEE.

At the end of the year 1845 we became engaged in one of the most serious struggles in which we have been involved in India. The country known as the Punjaub, in the north of India, was inhabited by the Sikhs, a proud and warlike people. The ruler of this country was friendly to the English, but was unable to manage the warlike troops raised by his father, who was known as the Lion of Lahore. He was assassinated by mutinous soldiers, and a new Maharajah or prince was proclaimed. The new ruler soon found that he could not manage the army any more than his predecessor, and that his only chance was to give it employment, and allow it to engage in a contest with the English.

The Sikhs, believing that they would be able to conquer all British India, declared war on the 17th of November, and in the following month crossed the river Sutlej into British territory. An army, under Sir Hugh Gough, advanced against them, and was attacked by the Sikhs, 40,000 strong, at Moodkee (18th Dec. 1845).

The enemy advanced in order of battle, with 20,000 infantry, 20,000 cavalry, and forty guns. The country was a flat plain, covered at short intervals with low thick brushwood, and dotted with sandy hillocks. The cavalry advanced to meet them, with five batteries of horse-artillery, and a cannonade commenced between the latter and the Sikh guns. Three regiments of English cavalry charged the vast mass of Sikh horse, and drove them from the field. The infantry pushed forward, and, after an obstinate resistance, drove the Sikh infantry from their position at the point of the bayonet, with great slaughter, capturing seventeen guns. It was late in the afternoon before the fight began, and the darkness alone saved the enemy from destruction.

On the 21st Dec. Sir Hugh Gough, largely reinforced, advanced against the great camp which the Sikhs had formed round the village of Ferozeshah. They numbered 60,000 men, and had 108 pieces of heavy cannon; the British were 16,700 strong, with sixty-nine guns.

Sir Hugh Gough directed the right wing of the army; Sir Henry Hardinge the left. The attack was made in the afternoon, the infantry advancing under a tremendous fire from the Sikhs' guns. Regardless of the hail of shot the men rushed on, carried the formidable intrenchment, and captured many of the guns; but the enemy's infantry, drawn up behind, opened so terrific a fire that they could get no further, so they fought till darkness came on and then lay down for the night. The fire had

Group of Sikhs.

been very heavy, and the 62d Regiment had seventeen officers killed, out of the twenty-three with which they went into action. All night the enemy kept up a fire of musketry and artillery upon the troops inside the encampment.

At daybreak the struggle recommenced. The British advanced with levelled bayonets without firing a shot, drove back the Sikhs, and captured the rest of the encampment. All thought that the desperate struggle was over, but in the course of two hours the enemy brought up fresh battalions, a large number of guns, and 30,000 fresh troops. Assisted by these they now drove in the British cavalry, and made a desperate attack on the British in the encampment. This, however, was repulsed, but in a short time still more Sikh troops and artillery arrived. The enemy's guns kept up an incessant fire, while the British guns were silent from want of ammunition.

Sir Hugh Gough then ordered the cavalry to charge both flanks of the enemy at once, while the infantry charged in front. The Sikhs were unable to withstand the assault. They abandoned their guns, and fled from the field. Thus 60,000 Sikh troops, supported by 150 pieces of cannon, were defeated by one-fourth of their number, British and Indian soldiers.

2. ALIWAL AND SOBRAON.

Sir Harry Smith was now despatched with 10,000 men and twenty-six guns to relieve Loodiana, which was besieged by the Sikh leader Rungjoor Sing. Having first relieved the city, he advanced to attack the enemy, who were strongly intrenched at Aliwal, eight miles distant, with 15,000 men and fifty-six guns. Here on the 28th of January, 1846, a great battle was fought. It was commenced by our horse-artillery, who galloped forward, opened fire, and silenced the enemy's guns, and thus enabled our infantry to advance without the loss that would otherwise have been occasioned. The British cavalry on the right made a successful charge, and one-half of the enemy's army was broken and dispersed; but on the left were the best Sikh regiments, and these fought with the greatest valour. They repulsed several charges of our cavalry, but they were at last driven back with the loss of all their guns but one.

While Sir Hugh Gough was waiting for reinforcements before crossing the Sutlej into the Punjaub, the enemy were strongly fortifying themselves at the bridge across that river at Sobraon. These formidable works were defended by 34,000 men on the one side, while at the camp across the bridge was a reserve of 20,000. As soon as Sir Harry Smith returned from Aliwal Sir Hugh Gough determined to attack the Sikh position. Some heavy guns had arrived from Delhi, and on the 10th of February, at half-past three o'clock in the morning, the British army advanced. The artillery were placed in a semicircle, and at half-past six the fog, which had obscured the view, rose, and a tremendous fire was opened upon the Sikh fortifications.

But the Sikhs returned the fire with seventy guns, and although their fortifications were terribly knocked about, they held firmly to them. Finding that the artillery alone could not decide the day, the order was given for the infantry to advance. Steadily they went forward through the tremendous fire, leaped into the ditch, mounted the ramparts, and captured the cannon. The Sikhs fought with steadiness and resolution. They turned several guns which were in reserve upon our troops, and repeatedly charged them with masses of infantry. Several times the British were driven back, but each time they rallied and returned to the charge until the second line came up, and the whole pressed forward together into the Sikh intrenchments.

The enemy fought to the last. Numbers, who had been pushed off the bridge as they crossed, were drowned in trying to swim the river, and fully a third of the Sikh army perished in the battle. Sixty-seven guns were captured, with all the enemy's munitions of war. The army then marched into Lahore, and peace was made with the Sikhs, who were allowed to retain a partial independence.

3. THE SIEGE OF MOOLTAN.

But the Sikhs, a proud and high-spirited people, were not yet convinced of their inability to resist the British forces, and during the next two years were in an unsettled and restless state. The position of the British officers who had been placed at the courts of their principal chiefs, with power to advise and to a certain extent to control them, was thus a difficult and even dangerous one. It was at Mooltan, where a young officer, Lieutenant Herbert Edwardes, occupied this position, that troubles broke out afresh. Mooltan, the chief city of the province of the same name, was governed by a Sikh called Moolraj. This person the government determined to supersede, and appointed another governor in his place. He was accompanied to Mooltan by two British officers and a body of native troops. Moolraj determined to revolt, won over by bribes the native troops who accompanied the commissioners, and suddenly set upon and murdered both officers.

The commissioners had had, however, sufficient warning of their danger to have time to write to Lieutenant Edwardes, who was with a small force at a place five days' march away. He collected as many men as he could and pushed on towards Mooltan, but on the march he learned that he was too late. He at once set to work to raise an army, and so great was his influence with the people that he got together a considerable force. With this on the 19th of June, 1848, he encountered the army of Moolraj, about 20,000 strong, and after a severe battle, lasting all day, defeated him, and drove him back into Mooltan.

On the 1st of July Moolraj again took the field and was again defeated. The city was surrounded and invested by Lieutenant Edwardes until a British army came up, and the siege began in earnest. The place was extremely strong, and defended itself desperately. On the 12th of September two British columns advanced to storm a fortified village outside the walls. The fighting was severe, but the enemy were driven out with a loss of 300 men. Just as the guns were ready to open fire and batter the town the news came that the whole Sikh army had joined the enemy.

Inspirited by the news, the enemy sallied out and attacked on the 8th of November, but were driven back, and a column under General Markham captured another position of the enemy outside the town after severe fighting. On the 2d of January, 1849, breaches in the wall were made by the British guns, and the troops marched forward to the attack. The Sikhs defended themselves desperately, but the British column fought its way in, and after a gallant struggle captured the town. Moolraj took refuge in the citadel, but was soon forced to surrender.

4. CHILIANWALLA.

In the meantime a British army under Lord Gough had marched against the army of the Sikhs, who were now in full revolt. After two serious skirmishes the armies approached each other at Chilianwalla (13th Jan. 1849). Here the Sikh chief Shere Sing had intrenched himself. After a heavy cannonade for an hour, General Campbell's division advanced against the enemy. The brigade of General Pennycuick advanced against one of the enemy's batteries, but the 24th Regiment, in its ardour to get at the enemy, left the native régiments with it behind, and was almost exterminated by the guns of the enemy and by the charge of the Sikhs.

One of the British cavalry brigades also suffered heavily, and would have been defeated had not its chaplain grasped a sword and shouted to the men, " My lads, you have often listened to my preaching, listen to me now! About, and drive the enemy before you!" Saying this, he placed himself at their head, charged, and drove back the enemy. The Sikhs at last retreated, but the English had suffered very heavily, and it was nearer a drawn battle than any that had taken place in India.

About a week later the troops again marched against the enemy, who had been joined by 1500 Afghan horse, and numbered 60,000 men with 59 guns, and were posted at Goojerat.

The battle opened, as usual, with an artillery duel, in which the British guns had the best of it, and the British infantry then advanced and stormed two villages in front of the enemy's lines. The artillery kept up with them and maintained so heavy a fire upon the enemy that they were unable to oppose any effectual resistance. Village after village was stormed, fifty-three guns were captured with the camp and baggage, and the whole Sikh army was soon in flight. The cavalry, who had during the battle effectually checked the masses of the enemy's

Shere Singh and his Suite.

horse, were now launched in pursuit, and for twelve miles
cut up the enemy and converted their retreat into an
absolute rout.   On the 11th of March the remainder of
the Sikhs in arms, 16,000 in all, surrendered.   The Punjaub was now annexed to India.

CHAPTER IX.—AN ERA OF REVOLUTION.

1. ROYAL VISITS.

While the country had been convulsed by political
strife, the private life of the Queen had continued un-
dimmed by a single cloud.   Her domestic happiness with
Prince Albert was perfect, and she had been very happy
in her family.   In 1844 she had intended visiting Ireland, but the unsettled condition of the country rendered
this inexpedient, and she paid another visit to Scotland
instead, spending some time at the castle of Blair-Athol,
placed at her disposal by Lord Glenlyon, afterwards the
Duke of Athol.   The royal family enjoyed their visit
greatly, the only incident of importance during the visit
being that the royal carriage was nearly upset close to a
narrow bridge in the Pass of Killiecrankie.

The royal party lived as private individuals, driving
or walking about quite unattended, entering into conversation freely with the peasants and others whom they
met.   During their walks the princess royal always
accompanied her father or mother upon a little Highland
pony.

In October the King of the French returned the visit
the Queen had paid him at the Chateau D'Eu.   Prince
Albert went down to Portsmouth to receive him, and

accompanied him to Windsor, when the Queen met him at the entrance.

The visit was a remarkable one, being the only one that a reigning monarch of France had ever paid to England voluntarily. The only other French king who set foot on English soil was King John, who was brought over a prisoner by the Black Prince after the battle of Poictiers, and who died at the building called the Savoy, in London.

The King of the French had seen many changes of fortune, and had previous to this time for years been an exile in this country. He told the Queen about the days when under the name of Chabot he was a teacher in a school in Switzerland, receiving the pay of twentypence a day. He scarcely thought that his adventures were not yet over, and that he was to end his days an exile in England.

After the French king had left, the Queen and Prince crossed to the Isle of Wight, and inspected Osborne House, which was then for sale. They were so much pleased with it that it was purchased, and became, as it still is, one of the favourite residences of the Queen. The house was taken possession of in the following spring.

In August, 1845, the Queen and Prince Albert crossed the Channel, disembarked at Antwerp, paid a visit to the Rhine, and stayed for a time with the King of Prussia at the royal palace of Bruhl on the Rhine.

The second son of the Queen—Alfred Ernest Albert, Duke of Edinburgh—had been born on the 6th of August, 1844, and on the 25th of July, 1846, the Princess Helena was born. In the autumn of this year a coolness arose between Britain and France on account of the marriage of the French king's son, the Duc de Montpensier, with the sister of the Queen of Spain. The British government did not want France and Spain to be connected in this way, and the King of the French had solemnly assured the Queen that this marriage should not take place. She was naturally hurt and indignant, therefore, that it should have been secretly arranged after the king's assurances to the contrary.

The Queen felt the matter more strongly that she had refused to arrange a marriage between the Queen of Spain and her cousin Leopold, solely because such a match was distasteful to the King of France. The matter caused a coolness between the two royal families and the two governments, for Guizot, the French minister, had deceived the British ministry as grossly as his royal master had deceived the Queen.

2. REVOLUTIONS IN EUROPE.

In the autumn of 1847 the royal family went to Scotland. They started from Osborne on board the royal yacht, touched at the Scilly Isles, and then sailed along the Welsh coast, past the Isle of Man up to the mouth of the Clyde. They now passed through the narrow channel known as the Kyles of Bute and on to Inveraray, where they were received by the Duke and Duchess of Argyll and the Duchess of Sutherland. They were drawn through the Crinan Canal in a gaily decorated barge, and went on to Oban next, visiting the caves of Staffa and the ruins of Iona. They left their yacht at Fort-William, and proceeded to the mansion which had been selected as the autumn residence for her Majesty. Here they remained for four weeks, the Prince shooting and fishing, the Queen riding and sketching, and the children scouring the country on their ponies.

The first ten years of the Queen's reign had passed quietly, all Europe was at peace, and there seemed no cloud in the air, but trouble was now approaching in various quarters. It began as usual in France, where the king had become personally very unpopular. A revolution broke out, a republic was proclaimed, and the king and royal family fled from Paris in disguise (1848). The king succeeded in escaping to England under the name of John Smith, and landed at Newhaven. The revolutionary spirit extended rapidly to other countries, and in Italy, Spain, Austria, and Prussia there were disturbances. In England there was also great agitation. An income-tax, which had been passed on a previous year, caused considerable discontentment. But the main cause was the distress among the working-class, and the addresses delivered at great numbers of meetings by the leaders of what was called the Chartist movement. This took its rise ten years before, and had steadily made way.

The demands of this party, as expressed in the document called the "People's Charter," were:—1. Manhood suffrage; 2. Annual parliaments; 3. Vote by ballot; 4. Abolition of the property qualification then required for members of the House of Commons; 5. The payment of members; 6. Equal electoral districts.

It was resolved that a monster petition should be drawn up, and that a meeting, in which it was calculated half a million people would take part, should be held at Kennington Common, London, and should march in procession to the Houses of Parliament.

3. THE CHARTIST AND IRISH TROUBLES.

Great apprehension prevailed as the day named for the Chartists' meeting approached. The police force was greatly strengthened; 170,000 special constables were sworn in, including almost every man of the upper and middle classes in London. Among them was Louis Napoleon, who afterwards became Emperor of the French, at that time an exile in England. Arms were supplied to the officials of the Post-office. A body of marines garrisoned the Admiralty; the Tower was put in a position of defence; the Bank of England supplied with artillery, and filled with soldiers. The Duke of Wellington had charge of the military arrangements, and concealed his troops in the neighbourhood of the various bridges so as to check the processions from crossing.

But when the great meeting at Kennington Common assembled (10th April, 1848) it was found that, instead of half a million, only about 30,000 persons came together. Only a small proportion of these had any idea of fighting, and the meeting gave up the idea of marching to Westminster. A few of the leaders were allowed to take the petition to the house. On presenting it they asserted that it contained 5,700,000 signatures, but when it came to be examined, and the list counted, it was found that there were less than 2,000,000. Of these also vast numbers were fictitious, and whole sheets of signatures were in the same handwriting. The failure of the meeting, and the ridicule caused by the examination of the petition, gave a blow to Chartism from which it never recovered.

In the meantime the state of Ireland was exciting great alarm. Mr. Smith O'Brien, the leader of the Irish party at that time, and his principal associates, openly avowed that they aimed at the establishment of a republic in Ireland under the protection of the French republic. As they were evidently preparing to take up arms to effect this object, and boasted that they would be assisted by a French army of 50,000 men, a stringent act for the suppression of sedition was carried. The insurrection broke out, but as soon as the troops marched against the insurgents the latter threw away their arms and fled in all directions. The leaders were taken, tried, and condemned to death. The sentence, however, was not carried into effect.

4. THE FOURTH VISIT TO SCOTLAND.

On the 18th of March, 1848, the Princess Louise was born at Buckingham Palace, and in the autumn of that year another visit was paid to Scotland in the royal yacht. This time the royal party were going to a residence of their own, for they had just taken on lease Balmoral Castle, on the upper course of the river Dee, in Aberdeenshire. The pressure of business during the time that the court resided in London was very great, and the Queen and Prince had benefited so much in health by their autumn trips to Scotland, that it was thought advisable that they should have a permanent residence there. The freedom and outdoor life enjoyed by the children was also extremely beneficial to them.

The stay in the north was this time a short one, for the royal family were back at Osborne in the beginning of October. On making the passage between Osborne and Portsmouth the Queen witnessed a sad accident. A boat containing five women was being rowed out by two watermen to the frigate *Grampus*, which had just returned from her station in the Pacific. The women were relatives of sailors on board, and were going out to welcome them home. A sudden squall swamped the boat, and all its occupants but one were drowned.

The following month Lord Melbourne, the Queen's first prime-minister, and her councillor and friend during the first years of her reign, died. On the 19th of May, 1849, another attempt was made upon the life of the Queen. It took place within a few yards of the spot where she had been already twice fired at. On her return from holding a drawing-room she had gone out for a drive with three of her children, and on her return down Constitution Hill a man standing inside the railings of the park fired at her. He was seized by the by-standers, and would probably have been killed by them had not a constable and park-keeper come up. He was tried at the Central Criminal Court and sentenced to seven years' transportation.

CHAPTER X.—THE EXHIBITION OF 1851.

1. THE QUEEN ASSAULTED.

In August, 1849, the Queen and Prince Albert, with four of their children, paid a visit to Ireland. The party travelled in the royal yacht, escorted by four men-of-war. They first landed at the Cove of Cork, where they were received with the greatest enthusiasm, which was repeated on their visit to Cork. They then re-embarked, and touching at Waterford, entered Kingston harbour, near Dublin.

The reception on landing here was one of the most remarkable of any that the Queen had ever received, and a no less enthusiastic greeting was given to the royal party in Dublin. After three or four days spent there the royal party again embarked, and paid a visit to Belfast, where the people of the north vied with those of the south and of the Irish capital in their reception of the Queen. From Belfast the party crossed to Scotland and journeyed to Balmoral, where they remained for six weeks. During this time there was a very serious outbreak of cholera in London, which carried off large numbers of people.

At the end of December the Dowager-queen Adelaide died, and on the 1st of May following the Queen's third son was born. As this happened to be the birthday of the Duke of Wellington, now eighty-one years of age, the duke's name was given to him, and he was called Arthur William Patrick Albert. The name Patrick was chosen as a compliment to the Irish, and as a proof of the Queen's grateful remembrance of the enthusiastic loyalty they had shown on the occasion of her visit.

Shortly after this another attack was made on the Queen. This was the only one of the attempts made upon her which was attended with the smallest success. The Queen had been to Cambridge House to inquire after the health of the Duke of Cambridge, and was getting into her carriage when Lieutenant Pate, a man of good family, sprang forward and struck her a blow on the head with his cane. The force of the blow was somewhat broken by her bonnet, but it inflicted a severe wound on the Queen's forehead. There seemed no possible motive for this attack, and at the trial of the offender his counsel could only plead that he must be out of his mind. He received, however, a sentence of seven years' transportation.

During the year 1850 preparations were being made for the Great Exhibition which was to take place in the following year. Prince Albert was one of the warmest supporters of the Exhibition, and took the greatest interest in everything connected with it. As president of the royal commission he managed to smooth away all difficulties, to bring over to his side many at first opposed to it, and finally to bring it to a successful issue. £64,000 were subscribed towards the expenses, and a guarantee fund of £200,000 was promised to meet any deficiency which might be caused should the receipts at the doors fall short of the expenditure.

2. THE EXHIBITION BUILDING.

The Exhibition was to be held in Hyde Park, London, and the great difficulty of the council was to make a choice among the immense number of plans sent in for the building. One was at last selected, but its great cost, the prodigious quantity of materials that would be required for the building, and its extreme ugliness, caused the committee to hesitate even after they had chosen it. Just after the selection was made a happy thought occurred to Mr. Joseph Paxton, the head gardener of the Duke of Devonshire. He had superintended the erection of great conservatories at Chatsworth, the duke's residence, and had been engaged on the construction of many other buildings of a similar structure. In reading in the papers an account of the difficulties that the committee were experiencing, the thought struck him: why not erect a palace of glass and iron large enough to contain all the articles likely to be sent into the Exhibition. He sketched out his ideas on a piece of blotting-paper which lay beside him, and was so convinced that they could be carried out that he at once took a seat in a railway-carriage and proceeded to London.

The committee, after some hesitation, and hearing something of his ideas, gave him a fortnight to prepare plans, and by the end of that time he sent in detailed drawings, and his scheme was accepted. Its advantages were: the quantity of light admitted, the extraordinary simplicity of the construction of the building, which consisted of nothing else but glass and iron, the facility with which it could be prepared, erected, removed, and re-erected on some other site if needful, the gracefulness of its appearance, and the ease with which it could be ventilated.

The building was to be 2100 feet long by 400 broad, and to cover twenty acres of ground. This great building was erected in little over six months, and the articles for exhibition were received and arranged by the day fixed for the opening ceremony, the 1st of May, 1851. Although there have since been many such exhibitions in different countries, some of them on a larger scale than this, none ever attracted so great attention or admiration. This was partly from the originality of the whole scheme, partly from the boldness and beauty of the building in which the Exhibition took place.

3. THE OPENING CEREMONY.

The Exhibition was opened by the Queen. The building was crowded from end to end, and decorated with the flags of all the nations whose arts and industries were represented there. There were assembled almost every Englishman of eminence, and numbers of illustrious foreigners. The Queen, amid great cheering, took her seat on a throne prepared for her, surrounded by the ladies of her court, the ministers of state, ambassadors from all parts of the world, and the high dignitaries of the Church. After the national anthem had been sung, Prince Albert, as president of the commission which had carried out the work, read their report to her. A prayer was offered up by the Archbishop of Canterbury, and the hallelujah chorus was then sung. The palace remained open until the 15th of October, and the Exhibition was, in all respects, a great success.

4. DEATH OF PEEL.—FRENCH *COUP D'ÉTAT*.

In politics a variety of subjects had occupied the attention of the nation during the years 1850–51. Sir Robert Peel died in the former year; his death being the result of an accident. He was riding up Constitution Hill, when he stopped his horse to speak to a lady. His horse, which was young and restive, suddenly shied and threw him off, and partly fell upon him. He was carried home; but, in spite of all that could be done for him, he died three days afterwards, to the great grief of all who knew him, and, indeed, the country at large. He was an upright and honourable statesman. His thoughts were devoted to the welfare of the country rather than the good of party; he was a staunch friend, and a gentle and forbearing opponent. The Queen fully shared the regret of her subjects at the death of the minister whom, since the retirement of Lord Melbourne from public life, she had come to regard as her safest and most trusted counsellor.

The Great Exhibition of 1851. View in the Transept, looking north.

At the end of the year 1851 Louis Napoleon, with the aid of the troops, overthrew the existing government of the French republic, after fierce fighting in the streets of Paris. A great outcry was raised against the violence of this proceeding, but if the republicans had the right, as they contended, to turn out the king if they were strong enough to do so, Louis Napoleon had an equal right to turn out the republic by the same means. This event caused some apprehension in England, as it was thought that Louis Napoleon might follow in the steps of his uncle, and try to wipe out the memories of Waterloo.

The idea turned out to be an altogether erroneous one. Louis Napoleon—the Emperor Napoleon III.—remembered the kindness which he had met with when an exile in England, and, from his accession to power in 1851 to his overthrow, nearly twenty years afterwards, he was the friend and ally of our country.

5. GREAT DISASTERS.

The year 1852 was marked by several lamentable catastrophes. In January the mail ship *Amazon* was destroyed by fire as she was entering the Bay of Biscay. There was a heavy sea at the time, and the flames having reached the engine-room the engineers were prevented from shutting off the steam; consequently the vessel continued to go ahead at full speed, and thus the lowering of the boats was almost impossible. The result was that a hundred and forty persons perished out of the total of a hundred and sixty-one on board.

In April her Majesty's troop-ship *Birkenhead* went down near the Cape of Good Hope, and, out of six hundred and thirty persons on board, only a hundred and ninety-four were saved. In addition to the crew, her passengers consisted entirely of officers, soldiers, and their wives and children. Never were the discipline and bravery of British troops displayed more brilliantly than upon this occasion. The soldiers were drawn up in line on deck with the officers at their stations, while the crew endeavoured to place the women and children on board the boats. Although the ship was sinking beneath their feet, the men neither faltered nor wavered, and she sank with these fine fellows standing in as unbroken array as if they had been on the parade ground. The scene is described in the following poem by Sir Francis Hastings Doyle, in the supposed words of one of the soldiers who survived:—

Right on our flank the sun was dropping down;
 The deep sea heaved around in bright repose;
When, like the wild shriek from some captured town,
  A cry of women rose.

The stout ship "Birkenhead" lay hard and fast,
 Caught without hope upon a hidden rock;
Her timbers thrilled as nerves, when thro' them passed
  The spirit of that shock.

And ever like base cowards, who leave their ranks
 In danger's hour, before the rush of steel,
Drifted away, disorderly, the planks
  From underneath her keel.

So calm the air—so calm and still the flood,
 That low down in its blue translucent glass
We saw the great fierce fish, that thirst for blood,
  Pass slowly, then repass.

They tarried, the waves tarried, for their prey!
 The sea turned one clear smile! Like things asleep

Those dark shapes in the azure silence lay
  As quiet as the deep.

Then amid oath, and prayer, and rush, and wreck,
 Faint screams, faint questions waiting no reply,
Our Colonel gave the word, and on the deck
  Form'd us in line to die.

To die!—'twas hard, while the sleek ocean glow'd
 Beneath a sky as fair as summer flowers:—
All to the boats! cried one—he was, thank God,
  No officer of ours.

Our English hearts beat true—we would not stir:
 That base appeal we heard, but heeded not:
On land, and sea, we had our colours, sir,
  To keep without a spot.

They shall not say in England, that we fought
 With shameful strength, unhonour'd life to seek;
Into mean safety, mean deserters, brought
  By trampling down the weak.

So we made women with their children go,
 The oars ply back again, and yet again;
Whilst, inch by inch, the drowning ship sank low,
  Still, under steadfast men.

—What follows, why recall?—The brave who died,
 Died without flinching in the bloody surf,
They sleep as well beneath that purple tide
  As others under turf.

They sleep as well! and, roused from their wild grave,
 Wearing their wounds like stars, shall rise again,
Joint-heirs with Christ, because they bled to save
  His weak ones, not in vain.

If that day's work no clasp or medal mark;
 If each proud heart no cross of bronze may press.
Nor cannon thunder loud from tower or park,
  This feel we none the less:—
That those whom God's high grace there saved from ill,
 Those also left His martyrs in the bay,
Though not by siege, though not in battle, still
  Full well had earned their pay.

A disaster of a different character took place in England by the bursting of a great reservoir near Holmfirth, on the border of Yorkshire and Lancashire. Nearly a hundred persons were drowned, seven thousand were rendered destitute, and the damage was estimated at £600,000.

In September the Duke of Wellington died at Walmer at the age of eighty-three. The whole country mourned for the great hero, and the Queen felt his loss very keenly.

The body of the duke was brought to London, and lay in state in Chelsea Hospital for four days, and he was then buried in St. Paul's Cathedral. The funeral was the grandest ever seen in London. Every regiment in the service was represented. Prince Albert, the ministers of state, the generals of the army, and a vast number of distinguished men followed him to the grave.

CHAPTER XI.—THE CRIMEAN WAR.

1. THE OUTBREAK OF HOSTILITIES.

During the year 1853 the prospect of war in the east of Europe had become imminent. Russia had always cast a covetous eye upon Constantinople, and the conquest and absorption of Turkey was the dream of every Russian statesman and soldier. In 1853 it was thought the time had come when Turkey could offer no effectual resistance to the armies of Russia. A flimsy pretext was made, and the Turkish provinces lying north of the Danube were seized by the Russians. It had, however, been a point upon which English statesmen of all parties were agreed, that it was the interest of England to prevent Constantinople from falling into the hands of Russia, and the unprovoked attack upon Turkey roused an angry feeling in England.

This was increased when the news came that a Russian fleet of six men-of-war and several smaller vessels sailed out from Sebastopol and, under cover of a fog, entered the harbour of Sinope where eight Turkish frigates, two schooners, and three transports were lying. The Turks were wholly unprepared for battle, and a great number of the men were ashore, when the Russians suddenly opened fire upon them. They hurried back to their ships, and fought gallantly against overwhelming odds. Every ship, with the exception of two, was destroyed by the Russians, and five thousand men were killed. The news of this event excited the greatest indignation, and the country strongly supported the government when the latter determined upon war in defence of Turkey.

The Queen had always taken a lively interest in her soldiers, and this feeling was naturally heightened when these were fighting the battles of the country. Previous to the departure of the troops for the east the Scotch Fusilier Guards marched to Buckingham Palace. The Queen with Prince Albert and her children appeared on

the balcony and waved a farewell to them, and the
men broke out into thundering cheers, waving their
bear-skins on their bayonets. As the war proceeded
the Queen took the most intense interest in the comfort
and well-being of the soldiers, and constantly wrote her-

Troops leaving for the Crimea.

self to Lord Raglan on the subject. Thus on one
occasion she wrote:—

"The sad privations of the army, the bad weather, and
the constant sickness are causes of the deepest concern
and anxiety to the Queen and Prince. The braver her
noble troops are, the more patiently and heroically they
bear all their trials and sufferings, the more miserable
we feel at their long continuance. The Queen trusts
that Lord Raglan will be very strict in seeing that no

unnecessary privations are incurred by any negligence of those whose duty it is to watch over their wants."

2. THE INVASION OF THE CRIMEA.

The French joined us against Russia, and on the 3d of January, 1854, the allied fleets entered the Black Sea. Troops were at once sent out; these landed first at Gallipoli, a town upon the Dardanelles, and in May moved on to Varna on the Black Sea. Here the army, consisting of about 22,000 English and 50,000 French, disembarked and prepared to move forward to the succour of Silistria, which the Russians were besieging. The Turks, however, defended themselves with such bravery, and inflicted such heavy loss upon the enemy, that the Russians gave up the siege and retreated northward.

For more than three months the army remained near Varna, the allied governments and generals not being able to make up their minds as to what should be the course of proceeding. The heat was very great, and cholera broke out and committed terrible ravages, especially among the French, who lost upwards of seven thousand men. At last it was decided that the army should cross the Black Sea and invade the Crimea. Unfortunately between Lord Raglan, the English commander-in-chief, and Marshal St. Arnaud, the French commander, there was little concert or agreement; and even when the whole of the great army was embarked, nothing was settled as to the landing-place. It was not until fourteen days had been wasted over a voyage which could have been performed in twenty-four hours that the landing-place was fixed upon, and the fleet arrived at the spot agreed on near Eupatoria. This delay gave the Russians time to move down their troops from Odessa and other places, and to prepare for an attack; whereas, had the voyage been made direct to the Crimea, they would have been taken wholly by surprise, and Sebastopol would have been captured without resistance.

3. THE BATTLE OF THE ALMA.

On the morning of the 14th of September the landing commenced, and by night-time the troops were all ashore. Both armies had received reinforcements, and the English contingent now amounted to 27,000 men. The next day the work of landing the cavalry and artillery went on; the lovely weather which had prevailed while they were at sea suddenly disappeared, and there was the greatest difficulty in landing the horses. On the 19th the advance began. The French marched next to the sea, the English by the side of them, while the fleet moved along the coast parallel with them, in readiness to give assistance with their guns. The enemy's cavalry presently showed in front, but upon our artillery opening fire they fell back, and the army halted for the night six miles from the Alma, where the Russians were, as was now known, prepared to give battle.

At nine o'clock next morning the army marched forward. The Russian position was on a range of hills rising from the river Alma; near the sea the hills were steep and difficult to climb, but inland the slope was more gradual, and was broken by vineyards and inclosures. The action was begun by the French division of General Bosquet, which waded across the mouth of the river and climbed the steep slopes beyond. The guns of the fleet had driven back the Russian defenders, and the French achieved their object without encountering any resistance. The enemy then brought up their troops to drive them back; but the French, with tremendous exertions, succeeded in getting a battery of guns up to the crest of the height and maintained their position.

As soon as this important point was won, the second and third French divisions crossed the river, and became fiercely engaged with the Russians who were in great force on the hill. Their fourth division came up to their assistance, and the Russians, unable to withstand their impetuosity, fell back. By this time the British were engaged. Until within a few hundred yards of the river the troops could not see either the river or the village on its banks, for the ground dipped sharply down to the stream. As soon as they reached the brow above the river the Russian artillery opened upon them, but the troops pressed on, dashed through the vineyards down to the water, crossed the river, scaled the bank, and pushed up the slope. It was impossible to maintain their regular order, the ground was so broken by hedges, stone walls, vineyards, and trees, but the British pushed on under a tremendous fire of musketry and artillery, driving the enemy before them.

4. BEFORE SEBASTOPOL.

The Russians, however, brought up reinforcements and fell upon the light division, which was in front, with such force that they were unable to hold their ground. But at this moment the brigade of guards and the Highland brigade came up in splendid order, and pressed forward through the storm of shot and shell until they were close to the Russian infantry, while the division of General

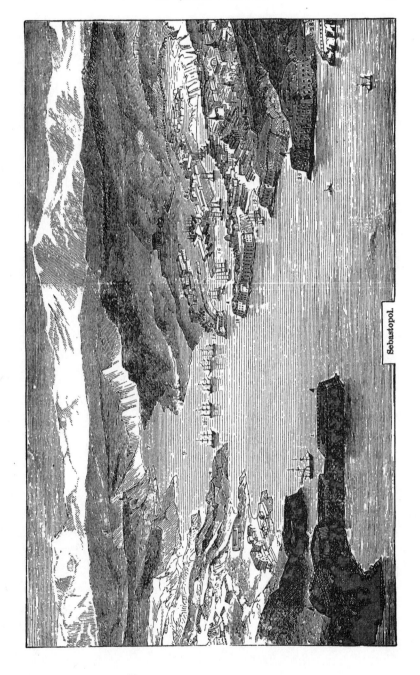

Sebastopol.

Sir de Lacy Evans on the right also won its way up the hill. The Russian soldiers, who had been assured by their officers that their foes could never climb the hill under such a fire as would be kept up upon them, lost heart as the lines of the allies reached them, and, giving way, retreated in confusion, while the allied troops occupied the crest of the hill they had so gallantly won.

The loss of the British amounted to about two thousand killed and wounded, that of the French was about eleven hundred and fifty, while the Russian loss was three thousand six hundred. Had the allied troops marched on at once against Sebastopol, the town would probably have been taken without resistance; but no move was made until the 23d, which gave the enemy time to recover from the effects of their defeat, and to prepare for resistance. It was determined to march round to the south side of the town, where the Russians, not expecting attack, would have made but slight preparations for resistance.

On the 26th of September the army took up its position on the heights looking down upon Sebastopol. The English occupied the harbour of Balaclava, the French that of Kamiesch, and the work of landing the stores and artillery at once commenced. The fortifications of Sebastopol facing the position the allies occupied were extremely weak, and could at this time have been easily carried by assault; but unfortunately the generals had determined upon regular siege operations. This gave time to the Russians to get up such formidable works that for many months they were able to resist the effect of all the guns that the allies could place in position against them.

Chapter XII.—TWO GREAT BATTLES.

1. THE BATTLE OF BALACLAVA.

On the morning of the 25th of October the Russians were seen in great force approaching Balaclava. Beyond the hills which shut in the little town a wide plain extended, crossed by a little stream called the Tchernaya, running into the head of the harbour of Sebastopol. The Russians had gathered in great strength on the Tchernaya, and advanced soon after daybreak upon four little redoubts or forts thrown up on the plain, and held by Turks. For a few minutes the guns of the redoubt farthest out on the plain played upon the advancing masses of Russians. Then the Turks, seeing themselves unsupported and threatened by a whole army, left their guns and ran across the plain towards the second redoubt. Few of them, however, ever reached it, for the Russian cavalry swept down upon them and sabred them.

Their comrades in the other redoubts shared the same fate, and the Russians then moved on towards Balaclava, now covered only by the 93d Highlanders, a Turkish regiment, and the English cavalry. The Russian cavalry led their advance, and as they came along in magnificent array the Turks fired a volley and ran. The Highlanders stood immovable. When the Russians came within six hundred yards a flash of fire ran along their front, but the distance was too great, and the Russians came steadily on, although the shot from the British batteries on the heights above Balaclava were plunging thickly among them. When within two hundred and fifty yards of the Highlanders another volley was fired, and so great was the effect that in another minute the cavalry were galloping back towards their infantry.

Lord Lucan now led the heavy cavalry brigade against a large body of Russian cavalry. Gathering speed as they went, the Scots Greys and Inniskillens who formed the first line rode at the heavy masses of Russian cavalry. Faster and faster grew their speed, till, with a mighty shout, they flung themselves upon the foe. For a time all seemed wild confusion to the spectators gathered on the heights. Then the red-coats were seen emerging from the rear, having cut their way through the surging mass. The Russians, however, were surrounding them, and it seemed that the little party would be annihilated, when the 4th and 5th Dragoon Guards, who formed the second line of the heavy brigade, burst upon the foe. Smitten as if by a thunderbolt, the Russian cavalry, men and horses, rolled over before the shock, and the column, shattered and broken into fragments, galloped away to the shelter of their infantry, while a shout of triumph rose from the long lines of the allies.

By the time that the British heavy cavalry had driven back the Russians, a strong force of the French infantry had reached Balaclava and the town was safe. An order was now sent to Lord Lucan by Lord Raglan to advance the light cavalry, but the manner in which Captain Nolan, the officer who carried the order, delivered it, made Lord Lucan suppose that he was to charge the enemy, and he repeated the order to Lord Cardigan, who commanded the Light Brigade.

Battle-ground of Balaclava.

2. CHARGE OF THE LIGHT BRIGADE.

The Russian guns were a mile and a half distant, backed by the whole Russian army, and the ground to be ridden over was swept not only by the fire of the guns he was about to charge, but by many other batteries on the flank. The enterprise was indeed a desperate one, but Lord Cardigan repeated the order, and the Light Brigade, numbering in all but the strength of a single regiment, set out at a trot. When at a distance of about twelve hundred yards from the Russians, thirty pieces of artillery opened fire upon them. Men and horses rolled over before the shower of shot, but the squadrons closed up the gaps and rode straight at the enemy, their sabres flashing in the sun, and leaving the plain behind them dotted with killed and wounded.

As they neared the battery the iron hail again swept the ranks, and then, with a mighty shout, they dashed upon the guns. The struggle here was short. The Russian gunners were cut down; and, gathering together again, the British cavalry rode straight at a Russian line of infantry formed up a hundred yards behind the guns. Unchecked by the volley of musketry poured into them, they hurled themselves at the Russians, and burst through their line. Their work was done now, but they were alone in the midst of an army of enemies. Turning, they swept back again through the guns on their homeward way. The flank batteries poured their shot into them, the rattle of musketry sounded around them; but they dashed all obstacles aside and rode on until they met the Heavy Brigade advancing to assist them and cover their retreat.

Our infantry now made a forward movement. The Russians fell back, and at half-past eleven the battle of Balaclava was over. The loss of the cavalry in this brilliant charge was forty officers killed or wounded and three hundred and eighty-six men killed and wounded.

3. THE BATTLE OF INKERMAN.

By this time great reinforcements had come down from the interior of Russia, two of the grand-dukes had arrived, and preparations were made for an attack, which it was hoped would drive the allies to the shelter of their ships. On the morning of the 5th of November, soon after five o'clock, the outposts of the second division, which lay on the right of the allied position on the edge of the plateau, perceived a gray mass moving up the hill towards them. Nothing had been done to strengthen the position; but although taken by surprise, and wholly ignorant of the strength of the force opposed to them, the piquet stood their ground stoutly until forced to fall back by the heavy masses of the enemy. General Pennefather, who commanded the division, hurried up his command, while Sir George Cathcart's division, and that of General Codrington also advanced to the front.

The Duke of Cambridge with the Guards moved forward and took up his post between the second division and that of Sir George Cathcart. There was no manoeuvring; each general led his men forward through the mist and darkness against the enemy, whose strength was unknown, and whose position was only indicated by the flash of his guns and the steady roll of his musketry. It was a desperate fight of individual regiments and companies, scattered and broken in the thick brushwood, against the heavy columns of gray-clad Russians who advanced from the mist to meet them. Few orders were given. Each regiment was to hold the ground on which it stood, or die there.

Terrible was the fight. Sir George Cathcart, with the 63d Regiment, was surrounded, and he himself and most of his officers and men killed. The 88th was surrounded, and would have been cut to pieces, when four companies of the 77th charged the Russians and cut a way of retreat for their comrades. In the second division the 41st was well-nigh cut to pieces. The 95th could muster but sixty-four bayonets when the fight was over. The Guards fought till their ammunition failed, and then with bayonets and volleys of stones tried to check their foes. For three hours this desperate fight lasted. As fast as one assault was repulsed fresh columns of the enemy came up to the attack.

Our ammunition was failing, the men exhausted with the struggle, their ranks melting away to nothing, and the day was well-nigh lost, when at nine o'clock the French streamed over the brow of the hill on our right, and fell upon the flank of the Russians. But even now the battle was not over. The Russians brought up their reserves, and the fight still raged. For another three hours the struggle went on, and then, finding that even their overwhelming numbers and the courage with which their men fought availed not to shake the defence, the Russian officers gave up the attack, and the battle of Inkerman was at an end.

On the Russian side some 35,000 men were actually engaged, with reserves of 15,000 more in their rear; while the British, who withstood them for three hours, numbered but 8500 bayonets; 7500 of the French also took part in the fight. 146 British officers were killed and wounded, and 2494 men. The French had 48 officers killed or wounded, and 1470 men. The Russians lost 247 officers killed and wounded, 4976 men killed, and 10,162 wounded.

Their losses at the battle of Inkerman had been so terrible that the Russians never again attempted to attack us, and the army now settled down to face the winter that was before them. It was one of almost un-exampled severity, and the sufferings of the troops were terrible. In the confident belief that Sebastopol would be taken before the winter came on, no attempt had been made to construct roads from the harbours to the front. The soil of the Crimea is deep and rich, and as soon as the rains began it became absolutely impassable for wheeled vehicles, for the wheels sank to the axles, and the cattle that drew them stuck fast and died in great numbers in the deep mud.

4. THE END OF THE STRUGGLE.

A misfortune befell the army in a terrible tempest which swept across the Black Sea on the 14th of November, dashing against the cliffs of Balaclava numbers of the merchantmen lying at anchor outside the harbour waiting until their turn came to enter and discharge their cargoes. Of the fleet lying there some half-dozen alone weathered the storm, the rest were dashed to pieces. The loss of life was very great. In one steamer alone, *The Prince*, nearly three hundred men went down, and the loss of stores intended for the use of the army during the winter was enormous. But the state of the roads was the chief cause of the terrible distress of that winter, and provisions were only obtained by the wearied men when they came off duty in the trenches marching down to Balaclava to carry up supplies. The want of firewood was almost more felt than that of food, and vast numbers of men fell victims to disease brought on by their sufferings.

THE ROAD TO THE TRENCHES.

Deadly road to deadly toil—thickly strewn with dead!
Noonday sun and midnight oil light the soldiers' tread.
"In the Trenches deep and cold, if I cannot save
England's glory, be it told—there I dug my grave!"
　　Faint the hero's voice and low—marching through the snow!

"Leave me, comrades! here I drop: on, my captain, on!
All are wanted—none should stop; duty must be done:
Those whose guard you take will find me, as they pass, below."
So the soldier spoke, and, staggering, fell amid the snow:
　　While ever, on the dreary Heights, down came the snow!

"Men, it must be as he asks: duty must be done:
Far too few for half our tasks, we can spare not one!

Wrap him in this—I need it less: soon the guard shall know:
Mark the place—yon stunted larch. Forward!"...On they go!
  And silent, on their silent march, down sank the snow!

O'er his features, as he lies, calms the wrench of pain:
Close, faint eyes: pass, cruel skies—freezing mountain-plain:—
With far soft sounds the stillness teems—church-bells—voices
      low,—
Passing into home-born dreams—there, amid the snow:
  And darkening, thickening, o'er the Heights, down fell the
      snow!

Looking—looking for the mark, now his comrades came;
Struggling through the snow-drifts stark, calling out his name:
"Here? or there? The drifts are deep. Have we pass'd him?"
      ...No!
Look, a little growing heap,—snow above the snow—
  Where heavy, on his heavy sleep, down fell the snow!

Strong hands raised him—voices strong spoke within his ears;
But his dreams had softer tongue:—neither now he hears!
One more gone, for England's sake, where so many go—
Lying down without complaint—dying in the snow!
  Starving, striving for her sake—dying in the snow!

Daily toil—untended pain—danger ever by:—
Ah! how many here have lain down, like you, to die!
Simply done your soldier's part, through long months of woe;
All endured with soldier-heart—battle, famine, snow!
  Noble, nameless, patriot heart—snow-cold in snow!
                                        —*Lushington.*

In the spring of 1855 matters mended rapidly. Ship-
loads of navvies and railway material came out from
England, and a line was made from Balaclava to the
front. Huts sprang up rapidly. Reinforcements arrived
from home; the sun dried the soil, and the aspect of
things became bright and cheerful. The duel between

the artillery of the opposing armies continued night and day, and there were many fierce fights in the trenches.

Early in June all was ready for the attack on Sebastopol, and a commencement was made by the French assaulting a Russian position known as the Mamelon. This they carried with a rush. Twice the Russians brought up great masses of troops, but the French maintained their position, while the British on their side carried some Russian works known as the Quarries. On the 18th of June an attack was made which would, it was hoped, enable us to carry the town. The French sent three columns, each six thousand strong, against the Russian work known as the Malakoff, which was the key of the whole position; but the Russians were prepared for the assault, and repulsed the attacks with great loss.

On our side twelve hundred men assaulted the Redan, but the ground in front of the Russian battery was so completely swept by the cross-fire of guns that few of the storming party ever reached even the foot of the enemy's battery. On the 16th of August the Russians attacked the French and Sardinians, the latter having now joined in the war. The allies were encamped on the plains of the Tchernaya, and their position was so strong that the Russians were repulsed with a loss in killed and wounded of nearly ten thousand.

On the 3d of September a tremendous fire was opened by all the siege guns of the allies, and was kept up until the 8th, when the assault was again made. The Russians this time were taken by surprise, and the French carried the Malakoff with a rush. The Russians brought up great masses of men, and for seven hours tried to recapture it, but in vain. In the meantime we had again attacked the Redan, but the Russians were now on the look-out, and a storm of shot and shell swept the ranks of the storming parties as they rushed forward. Nevertheless the British pressed on and got into the Russian work. The enemy, however, brought up such numbers of men, and opened so tremendous a fire, that our troops were unable to advance further; after an hour and a half of slaughter the survivors of the storming party fell back to their own lines, the loss being even greater than it was at Inkerman.

But the fighting was now over, for the capture of the Malakoff had rendered it impossible to continue the defence, and that night the Russians set fire to the town, blew up the forts, and crossed the harbour to the north side. No more fighting took place during the winter; in February, 1856, an armistice was concluded, and after long negotiations peace was finally signed.

CHAPTER XIII.—DOMESTIC EVENTS.

1. THE QUEEN AND HER SOLDIERS.

During the war the Queen paid several visits to the hospitals at which the sick and wounded sent home were lying, and as she moved along had a kind word for each of the patients. Upon one occasion the Queen herself distributed medals to some of the disabled soldiers, most of those selected for the honour having particularly distinguished themselves. Most of the gallant fellows had lost a limb, some more than one, and several had to be wheeled past her in chairs.

The Queen and Prince reviewed the troops at Aldershot on the 18th of April, 1856, and again in July, by which time the troops had returned from the Crimea.

Upon that occasion the officers and four men from each regiment which had been engaged in the field were ordered to step forward, and the Queen standing up in her carriage addressed them as follows:—

The Queen reviewing Troops.

"Officers, non-commissioned officers, and soldiers, I wish personally to convey through you to the regiments assembled here this day my hearty welcome on their return to England in health and full efficiency. Say to them that I have watched anxiously over the difficulties and hardships which they have so nobly borne, that I have mourned with deep sorrow for the brave men who have fallen in their country's cause, and that I have felt proud of that valour which with their gallant allies they have displayed on every field. I thank God that your dangers are over, while the glory of your deeds remains; but I know that should your services be again required you will be animated with the same devotion which in the Crimea has rendered you invincible."

On the 26th of June in the following year the Queen distributed in Hyde Park Victoria crosses to sixty-two officers and men who had distinguished themselves specially by deeds of valour. The order of the Victoria Cross had but shortly before been instituted, and the cross of valour is rightly considered the highest honour that a soldier can win. The crosses were of bronze and were made from the metal of cannon captured at Sebastopol. A great assemblage of spectators was present. The heroes of the day came forward singly, and the Queen presented and pinned on the crosses. These occasions were a few only out of the many in which the Queen has manifested a deep interest in her soldiers, and during every war in which they have been since engaged she has exhibited the greatest anxiety for their welfare, the greatest interest in their doings.

2. THE EMPEROR AND EMPRESS OF THE FRENCH.

The fact that British and French soldiers were fighting side by side in the Crimea naturally drew the countries closer together, and in April, 1855, the Emperor and Empress of the French paid a visit to the Queen. They were received by her at Windsor, and she has herself recorded her impressions of the first meeting: "I advanced and embraced the emperor, who received two salutes on either cheek from me and first kissed my hand. I next embraced the very gentle, graceful, and evidently very nervous empress. We presented the princes (the Duke of Cambridge and the Prince of Leiningen), and our children, Vickey with very alarmed eyes making very low courtesies. The emperor embraced Bertie, and then we went upstairs, Albert leading the empress, who in the most engaging manner refused to go first, but at length with graceful reluctance did so, the emperor leading me, and expressing his great gratification at being here and seeing me and admiring Windsor."

The Queen was greatly pleased with the empress, and described her as full of courage and liveliness, yet gentle and innocent, and with "the prettiest and most modest manner." The friendship thus commenced between the royal ladies has continued unbroken until the present day, and in the saddest hours of her life the empress found in the Queen a tender comforter. Little could either of them have foreseen, on the occasion of their first meeting at Windsor, that the time would come when one of them would be an exile in the dominions of the other. Little could either have thought that Queen Victoria would one day pour words of comfort and consolation into the ear of the Empress Eugenie on the death of her son, who died fighting bravely against the enemies of Britain in an obscure corner of South Africa.

The emperor and empress had an excellent reception in England. There were reviews and balls in their honour. The lord-mayor and corporation gave a great banquet to them in the Guildhall, there was a state visit to the Italian Opera House, and the Queen and Prince Albert accompanied the emperor and empress to the Crystal Palace.

On the 18th of August the Queen, with Prince Albert, the Prince of Wales, and the princess royal, returned the visit. Four hundred and thirty-three years had passed since an English sovereign had been in the capital of France, and the visit was considered to mark the end of the ill-feeling and rivalry which had for so many centuries existed between the two kingdoms.

The royal party were met at Boulogne by the emperor and proceeded at once to Paris, where the palace of St. Cloud was placed at their disposal. A week was spent in festivities of all kinds—reviews, fêtes, visits to the opera, and a magnificent ball given by the municipality of Paris in honour of the royal visitors. The enthusiasm which had been exhibited in London for the Emperor and Empress of the French was surpassed by that manifested in France for our Queen. On her return to England the Queen wrote an official letter expressive of her feelings on the subject of her visit to France.

"The Queen is profoundly sensible of the kindness with which she has been received by the emperor and empress, and of those manifestations of respect and cordiality on the part of the French nation by which she has everywhere been greeted. On personal and political grounds the visit to Paris has afforded the highest gratification to her Majesty."

3. LIFE AT OSBORNE.

During the two years of warfare the life of the royal family had proceeded in its usual quiet and domestic way. At Osborne the Queen had built a Swiss cottage in the grounds for their special benefit. Each of the children had a flower and vegetable garden, and each worked their best in friendly rivalry. There was a carpenter's shop in the cottage, and here the young princes were taught to use their hands. Part of the ground-floor was fitted up as a, kitchen with dairy and larder, and here the princesses were taught cooking, the making of pastry and preserves, and the management of a dairy. Their education was extremely thorough, and they worked more hours a day at their lessons than do most boys and girls at school.

Even on their walks and rambles their instruction was continued. They were taught to make collections of plants, insects, and geological specimens, and to arrange them scientifically in their museum. Their youth was a far happier one than that of the Queen had been, for hers was a solitary childhood, cut off as she was from all playmates of the same age, while they were numerous enough to form a good-sized party. They had, moreover, the constant care and companionship of their father, who, although strict as to their attention to their studies, was in all other respects one of the kindest and most indulgent of parents.

The princess royal was confirmed on the 20th of March, 1856, at Windsor. She had in the previous autumn become engaged to Prince Frederick William of Prussia. In May she met with an accident which might well have proved fatal: she was in the act of sealing a letter when her muslin sleeve caught fire. Fortunately the Princess Alice and her governess were in the room, and with great presence of mind they wrapped the hearth-rug round the princess royal and extinguished the fire. The arm was severely burnt from the elbow to the shoulder, but she showed great self-possession and uttered no cry from first to last. Her first thought after the fire was extinguished was of her mother, and she said to her sister: "Don't frighten mamma, send for papa first."

In the autumn of that year the Queen and the royal family for the first time took possession of the new house at Balmoral, which has ever since, for some part

Happy Days at Osborne.

of the year, been the abode of her Majesty. This was actually the property of Prince Albert, who purchased it from his private means as the Queen did Osborne. He specially left it to her in his will.

In November, 1856, the Queen heard of the death of her half-brother the Prince of Leiningen. On the 14th of April, 1857, the Queen's ninth child, Princess Beatrice, was born, and a few days later the Duchess of Gloucester, the last of the children of George III., died in her 85th year. At the meeting of Parliament the approaching marriage of the princess royal with Prince Frederick William of Prussia was formally announced, and Parliament voted her a dowry of £40,000 and an annuity of £8000.

4. MARRIAGE OF THE PRINCESS ROYAL.

Towards the close of July, 1857, Prince Albert went over to Brussels to attend the marriage of the Queen's cousin, Princess Charlotte of Belgium, and the Archduke Maximilian of Austria. The marriage was deemed likely to be a most happy one, and the young couple were fondly attached to each other, but it had a terrible ending. Some years afterwards the Emperor Napoleon went to war with Mexico, and the French easily overpowered all opposition. The emperor invited the Archduke Maximilian to accept the crown of Mexico. He accepted the offer and went out with the Princess Charlotte. The expense of the French occupation of Mexico caused great discontent in France, and the emperor suddenly recalled his troops, leaving the new king without the aid and protection which he had been given to expect. The result was that an insurrection took place, Maximilian was seized and shot, and the terrible scenes through which she passed unsettled the reason of his wife, who has been ever since insane.

The Queen's affection for Prince Albert, and the way in which she looked to him on all occasions, are shown by a letter written by her to King Leopold during the prince's short absence. "You cannot think how much this costs me, or how completely forlorn I am and feel when he is away, or how I count the hours till he returns. All the numerous children are as nothing to me when he is away. It seems as if the whole life of the house and home were gone."

On the 25th of January, 1858, the wedding of the princess royal to Prince Frederick William of Prussia took place. It was celebrated in the Chapel Royal, St. James's. In addition to all the royal family, King Leopold of Belgium, and the King and Queen of Prussia, Prince Frederick William's uncle and aunt, were present. For at the time of the marriage the prince's father was not yet king of Prussia, though he, as well as Prince Frederick William, have since been kings of that country and emperors of Germany. The princess's train was borne by eight bridesmaids, all daughters of noble families. The Queen felt the parting with her daughter very much. It was the first break in the family. The Princess Alice henceforth became the constant companion of her mother.

CHAPTER XIV.—THE INDIAN MUTINY.

1. THE OUTBREAK AT MEERUT.

Early in the spring of 1857 there were rumours of disaffection among the native troops or sepoys in India. From our first establishment in that country the East India Company had maintained a force composed of natives officered by Englishmen. As our possessions had grown so had this force increased until it had become a great army, or rather three armies, for the forces of the presidencies of Madras, Bombay, and Bengal were kept separate. It was in the Bengal army that the feeling of disaffection principally spread. The native troops believed that the time had come when they could easily drive the British out of India and re-establish the native monarchies. Evil-disposed persons went from

Sepoys of Bengal Army.

regiment to regiment exciting them to mutiny. One of the stories circu-lated among the troops was that the cartridges served out to them had been greased with pigs' and cows' fat in order to destroy their religion, the pig being an unclean animal to the Mo-hammedans, and the cow being sa-cred to the Hindus. Several acts of in-subordination took place, and the be-haviour of two or three of the regiments was so mutinous that they were disbanded.

The first serious outbreak occurred at Meerut on the 10th May, 1857, when the native troops rose in mutiny, murdered their officers, and all the Europeans, men, women, and children, they could find, and marched upon Delhi, thirty-two miles distant. In that city, the ancient capital of India, there was a large white population, but no English troops were stationed there. The consequence was that on the arrival of the mutineers from Meerut the native troops joined them and a terrible scene of murder and atrocity took place, the whole of the white population inside the walls of Delhi being murdered under circumstances of the most horrible and revolting cruelty.

The magazine in the city was held by three British officers and six non-commissioned officers, and was nobly defended until the little band were all wounded. Then the order was given, and the trains of powder they had laid were fired, and the magazine blown up, killing some 2000 of the mutineers and rabble of the town. The three officers and one of the non-commissioned officers survived the explosion and effected their retreat in the confusion through a small gate.

2. THE DEFENCE OF CAWNPORE.

The signal given at Meerut spread like wildfire. At station after station the sepoys of the Bengal army rose in mutiny, murdered their officers and all the white men, women, and children, and from the Punjaub down to Calcutta the country was in a flame. Only in places such as Agra, Allahabad, and Benares, where British troops were stationed, did we retain a footing, while at Cawnpore and Lucknow, in the newly-annexed province of Oude, the white garrisons were besieged. At Cawnpore the officer in command was Sir Hugh Wheeler, who had with him only fifty-five men of the 32d Regiment, the civilians belonging to the station, and those who had come in from outlying places.

It was hoped that there was no danger here, for Nana Sahib, a great native prince who lived close by, had been regarded as a great friend of the British, being profuse in his hospitality to the officers of the garrison and on the best possible terms with them.   Just before the outbreak a few British troops arrived from Allahabad, and when the revolt of the native troops began there were altogether 240 officers, soldiers, and civilians capable of bearing arms, and these had under their charge no less than 870 women and children.   A message was sent to Nana Sahib asking for aid, but his true character was now seen.   He at once, with his own forces, joined the mutineers, and assuming the command, advanced to besiege the hastily thrown up intrenchments of the British.

All the native Christians, with their wives and families, in the city of Cawnpore were murdered, as were many of the peaceable and wealthy inhabitants.   The bombardment of the British position was kept up day and night, and the sufferings of the besieged were frightful.   There was but one well, and the enemy concentrated their fire upon this night and day, so that it might be said that every bucket of water cost a man's life.   Red-hot shell were fired, and the building used as the hospital set on fire, and fifty sick and wounded burned there.   The other buildings were so riddled with shot and shell that they afforded scarcely any shelter, and the mortality among the women and children from fever and sunstroke was even greater than that caused by the missiles of the enemy.   Yet, although the army of the Nana was now increased to upwards of 12,000 men by the arrival of mutineers from other stations, the handful of Britons repulsed every attack upon their lines.

At last, after twenty-two days of obstinate fighting, the Nana offered a free passage to the defenders if they would surrender the place with its guns and treasure. As further resistance had become all but impossible the terms were accepted, the Nana and his Hindu officers taking the Hindu oath and the Mohammedans swearing on the Koran that the conditions should bo observed.

3. THE MASSACRE.

The women and children, the sick and wounded, took their places in waggons sent by the Nana, and the men marched besido them to the water-side, where seventeen or eighteen boats had been collected for their passage down the Ganges. The bank of the river was at this point rather high and covered with thick brushwood.

The wounded and sick were carried down the bank and placed in the boats; the men, women, and children took their places beside them. When all was ready the native boatmen were told to come ashore to receive their wages. Then, as if by magic, a terrific fire of musketry and cannon was opened from the bushes upon the boats. Numbers of the fugitives were at once killed, some, pushing the boats afloat, made for the opposite shore, but there also enemies had been posted, and with the exception of two or three boats which had drifted down the stream, all were sunk or captured. The men who were still alive were at once taken on shore and shot, the women and children, many of them bleeding from wounds, were taken captives into the town. The boats that escaped were seized by the mutineers at a place lower down the river and the occupants murdered.

Shortly after this treacherous deed General Havelock

with a little force of 1400 men fought his way up from Allahabad, defeating the mutineers and Nana Sahib's troops, until they reached Cawnpore, rejoicing in the

Well at Cawnpore.

hope of rescuing the hapless women and children confined there.

But when they reached the town they found they were

too late. No welcome greeted them at the house in which the prisoners had been confined. The leading officers entered the court-yard; all was quiet, but fragments of dresses, children's shoes, and other signs of English occupation lay scattered about. Entering the house the officers found the floor black with blood, the walls everywhere sprinkled with it, fragments of clothes, tresses of long hair, children's shoes with the feet still in them, a thousand terrible mementos of the butchery which had taken place met their eye.

It was soon found that the great well near the house was choked to the brim with the bodies of women and children. All the survivors of the first massacre, with some seventy or eighty women and children, fugitives from Futtyghur, who had been seized as they came down the river in boats, had been murdered by the orders of the Nana as soon as he received the news of the defeat of his troops by General Havelock's column.

The soldiers, who had struggled against heat and fatigue and a host of foes to reach Cawnpore, broke down and cried like children at the terrible sight. After that they went into battle crying to each other, "Remember the ladies!—Remember the babies!" and to the end of the war no quarter was henceforth shown to a sepoy.

4. THE SIEGE OF LUCKNOW.

It was not till the 30th of May that the mutiny had broken out at Lucknow, the capital of Oude. Sir Henry Lawrence, who commanded, had taken every precaution, and when the native regiments rose and killed all their officers upon whom they could lay their hands, the white troops marched against them and drove them off. All the European residents in Lucknow came into the lines thrown up round the Residency. Matters remained quiet until the 30th of June, when a body of 8000 mutineers approached the town. A small force went out to meet them, but were driven in again with heavy loss, and the siege then began. The garrison consisted of a few hundred British troops and civilians, and about 150 men who remained faithful from the sepoy regiments. These had under their charge over 1000 women and children.

The ground that they defended was a little elevated and close to the river. The Residency stood in the centre, and at a distance of some two hundred yards round it were grouped a number of buildings occupied by the garrison and connected by intrenchments of earth. This little inclosure has become memorable to all time as the scene of the most gallant and successful defence ever offered by a small body of men to an enormously superior enemy. The siege began unfortunately, for on the second day Sir Henry Lawrence was mortally wounded by a shell which entered the room in which he was writing. The command then devolved upon Colonel Inglis of the 32d Regiment.

Day and night the bombardment continued till the houses were riddled with shot and shell. The enemy made frequent attacks in heavy masses upon the intrenchments, but they were always repulsed by the garrison, every one of whom fought as if the whole defence of the place depended upon his individual bravery. Soldiers, civilians, and natives vied with each other in the bravery with which they performed their duty. The women too displayed an heroic patience and fortitude under the dangers and sufferings they underwent, for nowhere were they secure from the shot and shell of the enemy. And so for weeks the siege went on, while English ships were bearing across the seas troops destined for the relief of their brothers and sisters so hardly pressed.

CHAPTER XV.—THE TURNING OF THE TIDE.

1. THE ADVANCE UPON DELHI.

While the garrison of Cawnpore, after a noble defence, had been massacred, and that of Lucknow, cut off from all succour, was obstinately defending itself, the eyes of India and of Great Britain were fixed principally upon Delhi. It was there that it was to be decided whether the British or the natives were to be rulers of India. Thither, after rising in mutiny and carrying out the work of murder, the sepoy regiments made their way, to gather in the ancient capital and to salute the aged king who dwelt there as the monarch of India. The British authorities were conscious of the importance of that point, and took their measures with a calmness and judgment and a resolute facing of the tremendous danger which showed the best points of the British character.

It was certain that no aid could be sent up from Calcutta, for the whole country between Delhi and that city, with the exception of the circles covered by the rifles of the little garrisons of white troops, was in a state of mutiny. In the north the sepoy regiments mutinied, and the newly-raised Sikh regiments were wavering. At this all-important moment the fidelity of two or three of the great Sikh princes saved British India. Fore-

most among them was the Rajah of Puttiala, who, when
the Sikh nation was wavering, rode into the nearest British station with only one retainer and offered his whole
force and his whole treasure to the British government.
Many other prominent princes instantly followed his
example, and from that moment Northern India was
not only safe but was able to furnish troops for the siege
of Delhi. The Sikh regiments at once returned to their
state of cheerful obedience, and served with unflinching
loyalty and bravery through the campaign.

Not a moment was lost, as it was all-important to make
an appearance before Delhi and so to show the waverers
all over India that the British were neither disheartened
nor alarmed. The main force to act against Delhi was
collected at Umballah. A smaller body from Meerut advancing to join this was opposed by a sepoy force from
Delhi greatly superior in numbers. The sepoys, carefully
drilled in the British system and led by their native
regimental officers, believed that they were fully equal to
the British troops, but, as soon as this, the first fight in
the field, commenced, they learned the difference. The
little British force, animated by a burning desire for
revenge, rushed on them with such fury that the natives,
astonished and dismayed, abandoned their intrenchments
and fled. From that time, although the sepoys often
fought with great bravery, they had no longer confidence
in themselves.

The two British forces now joined and advanced towards
Delhi. The sepoys had thrown up strong intrenchments
and opened a heavy fire. The British did not wait to
return it, but with a tremendous cheer rushed forward,
and the sepoys were seized with a panic and fled, leaving

their cannon behind, and were joined by those stationed in a still stronger position in the rear. At nine o'clock in the morning of the 8th of June the British flag was planted on a steep craggy hill called the Ridge, almost

The Flagstaff Tower, Delhi.

looking down upon Delhi. As the flag floated out a thrill of anxiety must have been felt by everyone in Delhi, from the king down to the lowest street ruffian. So long as it waved it was a proof that the British rule was not yet overthrown, and that the day of reckoning and punishment would surely come for the blood-stained city.

The great importance of this contest was seen on both sides. The mutineers as well as the British felt it, and while the one never relaxed their desperate efforts to drive back the besiegers, the other held on against all odds, while scores of native chiefs hesitated as to which side they should join.

2. THE SIEGE OF DELHI.

The operations before Delhi were called the siege of Delhi, but should rather have been called the siege of the Ridge, for it was our force rather than that of the enemy which was besieged. Never before in the history of the world did 3000 men sit down before a great city, inhabited by a quarter of a million bitterly hostile inhabitants, and defended moreover by strong walls, powerful artillery, and a well drilled and disciplined force. The sepoy troops amounted at first to some 10,000 men, but were swelled later on, as the regiments of mutineers arrived from all sides, to 30,000 men.

No sooner had the British taken up their post on the Ridge than the sepoys sallied out to attack them. From that time till the end of the siege, nearly three months afterwards, almost incessant attacks were made upon the British position, each fresh regiment of the mutineers, as they arrived, heading the attack. But all was in vain, and at the end of three months the British flag still waved on the Ridge. At first the mutineers were elated with their success all over that part of India, and confident that the British rule was at an end; but in time doubts whether their mutiny and treachery would meet with final success, and fear that punishment for their atrocities would overtake them, began to enter their minds.

Pestilence broke out in the city, and a reign of terror prevailed there. The respectable inhabitants were robbed and murdered, and violence and riot reigned supreme. It was not till the 8th of September that guns fit for siege work reached the British camp, and the work of throwing up batteries began. Our men worked with tremendous energy, and as each battery was armed it opened fire upon the walls. In spite of the resistance of the enemy, and the fire of their guns, by the 13th great gaps were made in the walls in two places, and orders were issued for the assault at daybreak next morning. The troops were divided into four columns, each of 800 or 900 strong, while 1500 were kept in reserve to aid where needed. The numbers of the besieging army had by this time increased to 5000.

General Nicholson's column attacked one of the breaches, and, rushing forward through a tremendous fire, dashed up the slope of rubbish and won their way through the opening in the wall. An equal success attended the assault on the other breach. The third column was to assault the Cashmere Gate; but here a deed had first to be done which should live in the memories of Britons as long as we exist as a nation.

3. THE CASHMERE GATE.

Before the assault could be made the Cashmere Gate had to be blown in, and as the column moved forward a little party ran on ahead towards the gate. It consisted of Lieutenants Home and Salkeld, of the Royal Engineers; Sergeants Smith and Carmichael, and Cor-

poral Burgess, of the same corps; bugler Hawthorne, of
the 52d Regiment; and twenty-four native sappers and
miners, under Havildars (or native sergeants) Mahor and
Sing. Each of the sappers carried a bag of powder. The
gate stood close to an angle in the wall, and from the
parapets above and embrasures in the walls a terrible fire
was poured upon them. When they reached the ditch
they found the drawbridge destroyed, but crossed one by
one upon the beams on which it had rested.

The sappers laid their bags against the gate, and jumped
down into the ditch to allow the firing party to do their
work. Many had already fallen. Sergeant Carmichael
was shot dead as he laid down his powder bag; Mahor
was wounded. As Lieutenant Salkeld tried to fire the
fuse he fell, shot through the arm and leg; while Sing,
who stood by, was killed. As he fell Lieutenant Salkeld
handed the slow match to Corporal Burgess, who lit the
fuse, and fell mortally wounded as he did so. Then those
who survived jumped, or were helped, into the ditch, and
in another moment a great explosion was heard, and the
Cashmere gate flew into splinters, killing some forty
mutineers who were behind it. Then the bugler sounded
the advance, and the column came rushing forward with
a cheer, and burst into the city.

But though the entrance to the town was won, the
work had only begun. Every street and house had
been fortified, and during the whole day the most desperate fighting took place. Day after day the fight
went on, our troops gaining ground slowly, and often
having to break their way through from house to
house. It was not until the sixth day that they had
won their way to the palace, which was a fortress in

itself. This, however, was taken with but slight resistance, the sepoys having by this time completely lost heart, and having gradually retired by the bridge across the river on the other side of the city. The British flag was raised over the palace, and the thundering salute of the guns, and the cheers of the troops, announced that the heart of the rebellion was broken and British rule restored (20th Sept. 1857).

4. THE RELIEF OF LUCKNOW.

While the desperate fighting in the streets of Delhi was going on, General Havelock and his force were fighting their way up to Lucknow. They advanced from Cawnpore, and, after three days' march through a tremendous rain, found the enemy in force at the Alumbagh, a palace a few miles outside the city. After a sharp fight they were defeated, and the palace taken. The stores and baggage, and a force large enough to hold it against all assaults, were left here. After a day to rest his troops, General Havelock advanced, defeated the enemy outside Lucknow, and then fought his way through the streets of the town to the Residency, arriving there just in time, for the enemy had driven two mines right under the defences. These would have been exploded next day, and in that case the fate of the garrison of Cawnpore might have befallen the defenders of Lucknow.

The severe fighting in the streets had, however, terribly weakened Havelock's little force, for out of 1500 men who entered the city, a third were killed or wounded before they reached the Residency. With so weak a force it was evident that it would be hopeless to attempt to carry off the sick and wounded, the women and children, through the army of rebels that surrounded them, and it was therefore determined to continue to hold the Residency until further aid arrived.

The siege of Delhi over, steps were taken at once to relieve Lucknow, troops were sent off from Delhi, and these, joined by some marching up from Calcutta, gathered at Cawnpore. Sir Colin Campbell, who had just arrived from England to take the chief command in India, joined them here, and on the 10th of November the advance began, the whole force being 2700 infantry and artillery and 900 cavalry.

The fighting began on the 14th outside Lucknow, when two palaces near the town were captured. The next day an attack was made upon the Secunderbagh, a building of strong masonry, standing in a garden, surrounded by a very high and strong wall. The enemy were gathered here in great force, and also in a great mosque close by. The sailors of the naval brigade brought their heavy guns close up to the walls and opened fire. A breach was soon made, and the troops burst in.

There were 2000 sepoys in the garden, and these fought desperately, but the soldiers, with the cry of "Remember Cawnpore!" were irresistible, and every mutineer in the garden was killed. Then the mosque was attacked; the sailors brought up their guns to within ten yards of the wall, the soldiers covering them by their fire, and the mosque was speedily captured. Gradually the troops won their way forward; the garrison of the Residency, delighted at taking the offensive after their long siege, attacked the enemy with fury, and carried building after building at the point of the bayonet, and on the 17th the heads of the two forces met.

But Sir Colin Campbell saw that it would be necessary again to retire until a force sufficient to crush all opposition was collected; accordingly the gallant garrison, with the women and children they had so long protected, were drawn off, and the force retired.

CHAPTER XVI.—POPULAR MOVEMENTS.

1. THE END OF THE MUTINY.

It was not until most of the bands of rebels scattered throughout the country had been broken up that the British army again advanced against Lucknow. Here were collected 60,000 revolted sepoys and 50,000 irregular troops, besides the armed rabble of the city, which had a population of 300,000 souls. But the army was far more numerous than that which had before attacked the town, and none doubted of success. The fighting was desperate in the extreme, but day by day the troops fought their way forward, carrying palace after palace. At last, in the middle of March, 1858, they captured the principal abode of the King of Oude, where an immense quantity of treasure was found by the troops.

From that moment the enemy began to leave the town in large numbers, but it was not until after another week's fighting that the whole of the city was won. The fall of Lucknow broke the neck of the rebellion. It was some months before the flying columns of troops scattered all the rebel bands, and restored order throughout the country; but this was a matter of detail, and with the fall of Lucknow the great rebellion was brought to an end.

Hitherto India had been governed by the East India Company, but it was now transferred from them and placed directly under the Queen, and became really a portion of her Majesty's dominions. It was not, how-ever, until many years afterwards that she assumed the title which she now bears of Empress of India.

The struggle had been one of the most tremendous ever waged, and the best qualities of our countrymen were never shown to brighter advantage than in the manner in which they everywhere defended themselves against enormous odds, and in the resolution, energy, and calm-ness with which they faced difficulties and dangers of the most appalling kind. A full history of all the deeds of courage and daring performed during the Indian mutiny would fill many bulky volumes.

Although on a previous occasion the arrogance of the Chinese had received due punishment, that people had recovered their belief in their own superiority, and began to behave in their old high-handed manner. The British and French fleets, in consequence, bombarded and cap-tured Canton. In the autumn of 1857 the Chinese sued for peace, which was agreed to. As usual they broke the terms, and in 1860 a British and French expedition landed at the mouth of the Peiho, attacked and stormed the Taku forts, which commanded the river, and advanced to Tientsin, when the Chinese again opened negotia-tions. While these were going on they treacherously seized a little party of civilians and officers, and car-ried them away captives. The army at once attacked and defeated the Chinese, and advanced against Pekin, the capital of China; but the Chinese were completely cowed, and attempted no further resistance. Possession was taken of a gate of the town, and the Chinese paid the money we demanded; but when it came to the delivery of the prisoners they had treacherously captured, it was found that these had been so barbarously treated that several of them had died, and the rest were in a terrible condition. As a punishment on the emperor

Macao Fort, Canton River.

his summer palace, outside the walls, containing wonderful treasures of art, was sacked and burned, and the allies then returned to the coast.

2. THE VOLUNTEER MOVEMENT.

In 1859 Lord Derby's Conservative government brought in a Reform Bill, but were beaten, and were succeeded by a government of which Lord Palmerston was the head. In the course of the next winter Mr. Cobden went over to

France at the request of the government, and nego-
tiated a treaty of commerce, by means of which a large
number of articles hitherto taxed on importation by one
country or the other were henceforth to enter the ports
either altogether free, or at greatly diminished duties.
This treaty largely added to the trade of both countries.

In the session of 1860 a bill for the abolition of the
paper duty, which had hitherto been very heavy, and
had been a great bar to the circulation of cheap literature, passed the House of Commons. It was rejected by
the Lords, but became law in the following year. The
loss to the revenue was considerable, but the benefit to
the public immense; and indeed from this date must be
reckoned the commencement of the spread of general
education by means of the diffusion of cheap and popular
literature.

The three years from 1858 to the end of 1860 were
uneventful ones to the Queen. In August of 1858 she
paid a visit to Cherbourg, in France, where a vast harbour
and dockyard had just been built. She was received
by the French emperor. A few days after her return she
paid a visit to Germany to see her daughter Victoria in
her new home. She was greatly pleased with her visit, and
at finding her daughter well and happy. The princess's
first child was born in January, the following year.
The rule respecting godfathers and godmothers is less
strict in Germany than in England, and the princess's
baby had no less than forty-two godfathers and godmothers.

About this time an angry feeling sprung up between
Great Britain and France in consequence of an attempt
being made upon the life of the emperor, which attempt

was planned by French refugees in London. Threats of war on the part of French military men excited angry feeling here, and as a reply the Volunteer movement was set on foot. It met with great success. Great numbers of men came forward, and volunteer corps were formed all over the country. The Queen held a levee of volunteer officers at St. James's Palace on the 7th of March, 1860, and a great volunteer review in Hyde Park, at which 20,000 men were present, in June. She also attended the first meeting of the National Rifle Association at Wimbledon in the following month. In August she held a similar review at Edinburgh, in which 18,000 Scotch volunteers took part.

3. THE PRINCE CONSORT'S ESCAPE.

After the return of the Queen from Scotland, she, with Prince Albert and Princess Alice, paid a visit to Coburg, where they were received by the duke and duchess, and the Prince and Princess of Prussia. They spent a quiet time, as the mother of the Duke of Saxe-Coburg and of Prince Albert had recently died. The Prince Consort had a narrow escape of a very serious accident while staying here. He was being driven in an open carriage, when the horses suddenly took fright and ran away. A short distance ahead was a level railway crossing, the gate was closed, and even could it have been opened the carriage could not have passed, as a waggon was standing there waiting to cross. Seeing that in another moment the carriage would dash at full speed into the waggon, the prince jumped out, and escaped with some severe bruises. The driver was thrown out and seriously injured.

In December, 1860, the Princess Alice was betrothed to Prince Louis of Hesse. In March, 1861, the Duchess of Kent, the Queen's mother, now in her seventy-sixth year, was seized with a fit. When the Queen, with the Prince Consort and Princess Alice, reached Frogmore, where she was residing, she was unconscious, and the doctors had

Royal Visit to Killarney

already given up all hope of her recovery; in a few hours the duchess breathed her last. She was buried in St. George's Chapel, Windsor.

In the course of the summer the Queen was visited by King Leopold and the Crown Prince and Princess of Prussia, for Prince Frederick William's father had, by the death of his brother, now ascended the Prussian throne. In August another royal visit was paid to Ireland. The Prince of Wales, who had taken his degree at Cambridge, and was now serving in the army, was stationed there at the time. A visit was paid by the royal party to the lovely lakes of Killarney, and on the conclusion of the stay in Ireland they crossed to Scotland and spent some weeks at Balmoral, and then returned to London.

4. TRADES-UNIONS AND CO-OPERATIVE SOCIETIES.

Here it would be as well to notice the gradual rise and progress of institutions which have done much to alter the conditions of the working-classes. The first of these was the establishment of trades-unions. These great combinations of working men had small beginnings, but they spread rapidly. Their object was to enable the workmen belonging to the same trade to combine together to resist what they considered oppression, to enforce certain rules relating to their labour, to afford relief to unemployed or sick members, and to arrange the terms on which they would work for their employers.

At first very wild hopes were entertained by the men as to the power which these combinations placed in their hands, and they believed that they would be able to dictate terms to their employers. Strikes took place on a very large scale; trade was seriously disarranged, and very great alarm was felt by the public as to the effect which these pretensions of the men to settle the rate of wages at which they would work would have upon the trade of the country. There was at first, too, a great disposition on the part of the trades-unions to exercise a tyranny over men who did not belong to them, and to force them to join their body. This was carried to the greatest length in Sheffield, where outrages and murders occurred, and a parliamentary inquiry was held in consequence.

In time things settled down. The men found that in the great majority of strikes they were beaten, as the employers were able to hold out longer than they could, and preferred waiting for years to working at a loss. In some cases the effect was very disastrous to the men. Not only were their earnings of years swept away, but their trade was permanently injured. One long strike almost entirely destroyed the ship-building trade on the Thames. Thus the men learnt that there were limits beyond which they could not force up wages. A law was passed which put a stop to the interference with, or molestation of, men who declined to join the unions; and these bodies, although still powerful, ceased to be alarming. Their effect has been to prevent unfair and arbitrary treatment of workmen, to render agreements between masters and men more easy, and in some instances to raise the rate of wages. Upon the other hand some branches of trades have been unquestionably injured by the fact that wages were kept up by unions to a point which enabled our foreign rivals in trade to compete successfully with English manufacturers.

Another movement which, while it had little influence in London, has much improved the condition of the working-classes in the north of England, is co-operative societies. The first of these was started at Rochdale on a very small scale, but increased until it became an immense undertaking. The object of these societies is to enable men of the working-classes to buy their food and other necessaries of life at cost price. This is done by subscribing money to open shops, at which all the members of the association deal, paying only the original cost of the goods, with a slight additional price to cover the expenses of the management.

Another movement of a most beneficial character has been that of building societies, which, by means of subscriptions, enable their members to purchase the houses in which they live. The establishment of savings-banks, and especially of the Postal Savings-bank, has also done immense good by encouraging saving habits, and helping the working-classes to improve their condition, and make a provision for old age. The same may be said of the friendly societies, which have been of inestimable benefit to the working-classes.

Chapter XVII.—DEATH OF THE PRINCE CONSORT.

1. THE CIVIL WAR IN AMERICA.

On November the 22d, 1861, the Prince Consort visited Sandhurst, and inspected the New Military College there. The day was a wet one, and he caught a severe cold. He also suffered much from depression when the news came next day that the young Queen of Portugal and some of the members of her family had been suddenly carried off by typhoid fever.

As yet the indisposition of the Prince excited no uneasiness. He had for the last fortnight been suffering from rheumatism, but on the 25th was well enough to travel to Cambridge to visit the Prince of Wales there. The next two days he was no better, and on the

28th his illness was aggravated by the news that the *Trent* mail steamer had been stopped on her passage to England by an American man-of-war, and that two passengers, Messrs. Slidell and Mason, had been taken out of her.

At this time the great war between the Northern and Southern States of America was going on, and these two gentlemen were on their way as commissioners from the latter to Britain. The news of this action on the part of the commander of the United States' ship caused a tremendous outbreak of indignation in Britain. Preparations were instantly made for war. The Guards were hurried on board ship and despatched to Canada, and an order was sent to the British ambassador at Washington to demand satisfaction, and if he did not obtain it, to leave the country at once.

Few hopes were entertained that America would consent to give up the prisoners so unjustifiably captured, for the American Congress had, as soon as the news was known, voted an address of thanks to the officer commanding the vessel that stopped the *Trent*. But happily the president and his advisers were wiser than the mass of the people, and saw that to provoke war with Britain at a time when all their energies were necessary to carry the struggle at home to a successful termination would be suicidal. They therefore repudiated the action of their officer, and restored the prisoners.

2. THE PRINCE CONSORT'S ILLNESS.

The news of this affair, and the excitement which it caused in the country, greatly affected the Prince. He used his utmost efforts to ensure that the order sent to the British ambassador at Washington should be in language that would render it possible for the American government to yield the point demanded without loss of dignity. Although still suffering much the Prince was able to go out until Sunday, December 1st, when he attended service in the chapel as usual. The next day his illness took a change for the worse, and a sort of low fever set in. The Queen was greatly alarmed, the news so lately received of the deaths in the royal family of Portugal naturally adding to her anxiety. The two physicians in attendance reassured her by telling her there was hope that the fever would pass off.

Each day, however, the fever gained strength. The Prince retained his calmness and composure, although he no doubt felt that he was sick unto death, for at the very commencement of his illness he had said that he was glad it was not fever, "as that, he felt sure, would be fatal to him." The Queen was almost broken down at the prospect of her loss, but Princess Alice showed the greatest composure and fortitude. She was the constant companion of her father, and by her calmness and example greatly strengthened her mother. On the Sunday, at the Prince's request, a piano was brought into his room, and the Princess Alice played and sang some of his favourite hymns to him.

The Prince himself had no fear of death. Not long before his fatal illness he had said to the Queen, "I do not cling to life. You do, but I set no store by it. If I knew that those I love were well cared for, I should be quite ready to die to-morrow." All his actions through life showed indeed that he was a man of sincere piety, and that religion occupied a very prominent part in his thoughts.

3. A WIDOWED QUEEN.

During the Prince's illness he spoke openly of his condition, and expressed many wishes as to arrangements to be made after his death. These were always spoken to the Princess Alice, for the Queen could not bear to listen to him, but the princess always retained her calmness when with her father or mother, breaking down only when alone. Other physicians were now called in, and although they regarded the case as very serious, they did not consider it hopeless. On the 12th of December the illness increased, and the Princess Alice summoned the Prince of Wales from Cambridge. There was a slight improvement on the following day, but on the 14th the change was again for the worse, and when the Queen asked the doctors if she could go out for a breath of fresh air, they told her not to go for more than a quarter of an hour.

Some hours passed without any further change, but even the Queen saw that death was near at hand. His last articulate words were "Good little wife," spoken in German. The children came one after another into the room, but the Prince gave no signs of recognizing them; and at a quarter to eleven, with his wife and children kneeling round him, he passed quietly away. Just at midnight the great bell of St. Paul's began to toll and spread the sad news of the Prince Consort's death over London. The telegraph sent the news all over the country. The following day was Sunday, and many learnt for the first time, by the omission of the Prince Consort's name from the litany, of the loss which the Queen and the nation had suffered.

For twenty-one years the Prince had been the wise adviser and support of the Queen, besides being a loving husband and an affectionate father to her children, and the Queen suffered terribly under the unexpected blow that had befallen her. For three days her state occasioned great anxiety to her medical attendants, and she was so weak that her pulse could scarcely be felt. For some time she absolutely refused to leave Windsor before the funeral. It was only upon its being represented to her that the fever which had proved fatal to the Prince might attack the children, that she gave way and started with the Prince of Wales and the Princesses Alice and Helena for Osborne.

The Prince of Wales returned for the funeral, which took place at Windsor on the 23d of December. The ministers, foreign ambassadors, the knights of the Garter, and many princes of foreign countries were present, among them Prince Albert's brother, the Duke of Saxe-Coburg. The only children of the prince present were the Prince of Wales and Prince Arthur. The Prince Consort was greatly mourned throughout the kingdom for his own sake and for that of the Queen. Mourning was generally worn for some weeks, and the grief was as deep and general as it had been at the death of the Princess Charlotte.

4. THE EXHIBITION OF 1862.

The year 1862 was one of depression. The civil war which was raging in America very seriously affected our trade with that country, and the fact that the supply of cotton from the Southern States was almost entirely cut off, caused a cessation of work in the greater number of the mills of Lancashire, thus bringing an immense amount of suffering upon the working-classes there. But a very large subscription was got up, and the factory hands were assisted to tide over the bad times.

The absence of the Queen at the opening of Parliament, the gloom caused by the death of the Prince Consort, and the cessation of all court entertainments and festivities affected trade in London. But this was to some extent counterbalanced by the opening in May of the second great exhibition, which was even larger and far more complete in all its branches than that of 1851, although the building was very inferior in beauty to that of the first exhibition. The building of 1851 had been bought by a company and erected at Sydenham, where, under the name of the Crystal Palace, it has ever since been one of the greatest attractions of London.

The absence of the Prince Consort, who had taken a very prominent part in all the arrangements connected with the new exhibition, and the contrast which the opening ceremony afforded to that of 1851, when the Queen and Prince Albert were the leading figures, had a very depressing effect upon all who were present.

The principal events affecting the royal family during the year 1862 were that the Prince of Wales took a lengthened tour in the East, and that on the 1st of July the Princess Alice was quietly married to Prince Louis of Hesse. Although the marriage had been delayed for some months in consequence of the Prince Consort's death, it took place at a shorter time after that event than would be the case in private families; but among royal personages family feeling has to give way to reasons of state.

On the 18th of December the body of the Prince Consort was removed from its temporary resting-place beneath St. George's Chapel, Windsor, to the splendid mausoleum which the Queen had erected at Frogmore. To this tomb the Queen and the members of her family in England have ever since repaired annually on the anniversary of his death.

CHAPTER XVIII.

MARRIAGE OF THE PRINCE OF WALES.

1. ARRIVAL OF THE PRINCESS.

The greatest event of the year 1863 was the marriage of the Prince of Wales. The interest of the people in this marriage was unbounded; it was known that the match was one of affection, and that the princess was one of the most charming in Europe. But the principal reason for the popularity of the marriage was, perhaps, that the Princess Alexandra was a Dane, one of the race from whom a considerable portion of the English people are descended. From our Danish blood we derive that love of the sea which is inborn in almost every Briton, which has rendered the country mistress of the seas, and spread her dominion far and wide over the world. For many years our royal alliances had been all German, and this reintroduction of Danish blood into the royal family was hailed with the greatest satisfaction by the people.

On the 7th of March the Princess Alexandra, accompanied by her father, mother, brother, and sister, arrived at Gravesend. The Prince of Wales was there to meet her, and she landed on English soil amid the tremendous cheers of a vast concourse of people. In London the excitement was immense; the streets along which she was to pass were brilliantly decorated, the united flags of Great Britain and Denmark waved everywhere, mottoes of welcome met the eye at every turn, and an enormous crowd assembled in the streets.   Triumphal arches had been erected in great numbers.

As the open carriage containing the Prince of Wales and the Princess came along it was received with enthusiastic cheering. Unfortunately the authorities in the city had not expected so vast a gathering, and the arrangements they had made for keeping the streets were altogether insufficient. The consequence was

Prince of Wales.

that the crowd, eager to approach the carriage and to obtain a near view of the beautiful young princess, broke the bounds and closed in round the carriage, cheering and shouting. So great was the crowding that several lives were lost, and the princess, unaccustomed to so vehement and uproarious a greeting, was almost frightened by the boisterous welcome with which she was received.

2. THE MARRIAGE.

The royal party drove to Paddington and then went down by train to Slough, near Windsor. Here they were met by the Princes of Prussia and Hesse and Princes Leopold and Arthur, and on their arrival at the castle the Princess Alexandra was received by the Queen and the Princesses Louise and Beatrice. The marriage ceremony took place three days afterwards in St. George's Chapel. The whole of the prince's brothers and sisters were present, together with the great officers of state and a vast number of distinguished personages. The Queen did not

Princess of Wales.

mingle with the brilliant throng in the chapel, but, dressed in her widow's dress, witnessed the ceremony from the royal closet, apart from the rest.

The princess's wedding presents were exceedingly numerous, almost every town in England having sent up jewels or other gifts to the bride of the Prince of Wales. The rejoicings were general throughout the whole country; every town was decorated; every church bell pealed out its joyful notes. The illuminations in the streets of

London were magnificent, and the crowd in the principal streets so tremendous that, as on the occasion of the passage through the streets, six persons were crushed to death.

The enthusiasm with which the Princess Alexandra was greeted upon her arrival in this country was no passing feeling. As the years have gone on the universal admiration felt by the people for the fair young princess, who was in the course of nature some day to be their queen, has never abated; while the charm of her manner, and the amiability of her disposition, have won for her a high place in their affections.

3. ACCIDENT TO THE QUEEN.

In the month of May the Queen and Princess Alice went over the military hospital at Netley, and conversed with many of the sick soldiers. In August she paid a visit to Belgium and Germany, and stopped for some time with her daughters Victoria and Alice and their husbands. In October, when the Queen was at Balmoral, a serious accident took place. She was driving with the Princesses Alice and Helena, and returning after dark the carriage upset. The Queen and her daughters were thrown out. The Queen fell on her face and was much bruised. The princesses escaped without injury. For a short time the confusion was great, as the horses had both fallen and were struggling to get up, and in the darkness none knew whether the Queen and her daughters had not been seriously injured. The traces of the carriage were cut to release the horses, and the royal ladies sat in the carriage until a servant arrived with some ponies, upon which they rode back to Balmoral.

Shortly afterwards the Queen took part in a public ceremony for the first time since the death of her husband. The occasion was the unveiling of a statue of the Prince Consort at Aberdeen. The Queen was accompanied by all her children, with the exception of the Prince of Wales, the Duke of Edinburgh, and the Princess Beatrice. It was a trying occasion for the Queen. The day was very wet, and the crowd who lined the streets of Aberdeen received her with respectful silence, which testified to their sympathy, but which must have struck her the more by its contrast with the enthusiastic greeting which she had always received upon occasions of state ceremony.

Towards the end of the year 1864 two men who had occupied very leading positions in the eyes of their countrymen passed away. The one was Richard Cobden, the leader of the free-trade movement; the other Lord Palmerston, who was one of the most popular statesmen in England. He owed his popularity less to his powers of statesmanship or to his genius than to his personal qualities. He was one of the most genial and good-tempered of men, and took the ups and downs of political life with a cheerful light-heartedness that there was no disturbing. No attacks by political opponents could ruffle him, and he never said an ill-natured thing of the most bitter political foe.

One reason for the regard with which he was viewed was the strongly patriotic attitude which he always took up when the honour or interest of the country was assailed abroad. He was in his eighty-first year when he died; but to the last he retained his activity, cheerfulness, and geniality. His illness began by a cold caught from riding imprudently in an open carriage without an over-coat. He died after an illness of a few days. At the special desire of the Queen herself he was buried in Westminster Abbey. He was prime-minister at the time of his death, and was succeeded in that position by Earl Russell.

In the following year there was a terrible outbreak in England of a disease called the rinderpest, which committed great havoc among the cattle, some 75,000 of which either died or were killed on the malady showing itself. The stringent measures which were taken were at last successful in stamping out the disease.

4. THE TEMPERANCE MOVEMENT.

About this time a movement, which was in the first place due to the generosity of an American gentleman named Peabody, began to extend. Mr. Peabody had been for many years a resident in England, where he had made a large fortune, and he determined to devote a large portion of it to the benefit of the poorer class of this country. In March, 1862, he placed in the hands of trustees for the benefit of the poor of London the sum of £150,000, and the following year he gave an additional £100,000. Later on he added another £100,000, and at his death he increased the sum total to half a million. With this large sum of money building sites were purchased and houses erected capable of lodging in comfort a very large number of families. The work so begun was taken up by others, and the number of "model dwelling-houses," as these buildings are generally called, is now considerable. They afford accommodation to a vast number of working-class families.

It was about this period of the Queen's reign that a movement which has had an immense effect of late years in bettering the condition of the working-classes and of lessening crime began to attain large proportions. In the year 1852 Mr. Nathaniel Card, a Quaker and a total abstainer from liquor, formed an association for the purpose of putting down the traffic in intoxicating liquors, and the association increased until it attained very large dimensions. In 1857 upwards of 3000 ministers of religion signed a declaration in favour of its principles. The first bill on the subject introduced in the House of Commons was in the year 1864, since which time many other bills on the subject have been brought forward, but always without success. The proposal that a certain number of persons shall be able to prevent all other persons living in the same district from buying in-' toxicating liquors is considered by many as interfering too much with the liberty of the people.

But although the league has not been successful in carrying such a law, its labours in the cause of temper-. ance have had a very great effect, and have been very largely assisted by the action of other bodies agreeing with them as to the evils of intemperance. The pressure for employment has in itself been an aid to the cause of temperance. Employers who can pick and choose will only retain the services of steady and sober men, and a drunkard can never long retain his situation. Thus the movement in favour of temperance has gone on steadily. The ranks of those who abstain altogether grow every year larger. The number of convictions for drunkenness as steadily goes down, and the figures of the revenue show an annual falling off in the consumption of liquor. It is earnestly to be hoped that the time will come when a drunkard will be viewed by his fellow-men with contempt and loathing as one altogether without self-respect, a bad husband and father, and unfit for the association of decent men.

CHAPTER XIX.—THE ABYSSINIAN EXPEDITION.

1. THE HYDE PARK RIOTS.

In 1866 the attention of the country was occupied by the question of reform of the franchise, or system of electing members of parliament. In the early days of Parliament members had been elected solely by the wealthier citizens of the towns and by the land-owners in the counties. The Reform Bill of 1832 had greatly extended the franchise, and had given the vote to large numbers of people who had before been without it. It had taken away members of parliament from many small and unimportant places, and had given them to the populous towns which owed their existence to the growth of manufactures. Mr. Gladstone now brought in a bill to carry this principle much further. He failed to get the measure passed, and a Conservative government came into power. Great meetings were held in many large towns in favour of reform. The most important of these took place in London, and was the cause of what has since been known as the Hyde Park Riots. The meeting was got up by two associations, the Reform Union and the Reform League.

Fearing disturbances would take place government determined to prevent the meeting being held, and a notice forbidding it was issued by the head of the London police. But those who had prepared for it determined to hold it in spite of government, and on the 23d of July an immense crowd assembled near the Marble Arch, forming one of the entrances to Hyde Park. The members of the Reform League, who formed but a very small portion of the crowd, made their way to the gate and formally asked permission to enter. This was refused, and they went in procession to Trafalgar Square, where they held their meeting.

But so peaceful a termination to the processions did not suit the crowd of roughs and disorderly persons assembled at the Marble Arch. They laid hold of the park railings and pulled them down. Then they poured into the park, overpowering the police by the weight of their numbers, trampled down the flowers and broke the shrubs, and did a great deal of damage.

The year 1866 was memorable for the successful laying of a telegraph cable to America. One had previously been laid, but had almost immediately broken down. The *Great Eastern* steamship was employed to carry the new cable, and not only was this successfully laid, but the old one was picked up and the break discovered and mended. In July of this year the Princess Helena was married to Prince Christian of Schleswig-Holstein. During the winter there was considerable distress in the country. The harvest had been a bad one, trade was greatly depressed, vast numbers of people were out of employment, and cholera and typhus caused large numbers of deaths.

2. THE FENIAN TROUBLES.

The year 1866 had been marked by another great war in Europe. Prussia and Italy had declared war with

Austria. At the beginning of the campaign the Italian army crossed the frontier, but were signally defeated by an Austrian force of inferior strength at the battle of Custozza, and the Italian fleet was also defeated by that of Austria at the battle of Lissa. In the north, however, the Prussian army completely defeated that of Austria, and marching upon Vienna compelled the Austrians to grant the terms demanded.

By these the power of Prussia was largely increased in Germany, while Italy gained Venice and that portion of Northern Italy hitherto held by the Austrians. Thus for the first time since the days of the Romans Italy became a united kingdom under a single authority.

At the meeting of Parliament in 1867 Mr. Disraeli brought in a Reform Bill which went considerably further than that introduced by Mr. Gladstone in the foregoing year. Some of the Conservatives objected to this bill, which they considered placed the whole political power throughout the country in the hands of the working-classes, but the bill was finally carried.

On the 20th of May the Queen, with all the members of her family present in England, attended the opening ceremony of the building in London known as the Albert Hall. This was at first called the Hall of Arts and Science, and was intended to benefit those branches of human knowledge in which the Prince Consort had taken so lively an interest.

In July the Sultan of Turkey paid a visit to England and stayed with the Queen at Windsor Castle. A grand naval review was held at Spithead; the Queen afterwards went to Scotland and paid a visit to the Duke and Duchess of Roxburgh at Floors Castle.

On the 18th of September some Fenian prisoners, that is, members of a secret society of Irish rebels, who had been brought before a magistrate at Manchester, were being taken to prison when the van was attacked by a number of Irishmen. They fired on it, killed one of the horses, shot the police-sergeant in charge, and carried off the prisoners. Great excitement was caused throughout the country. Three of the men who had headed the attack were captured, tried, and hung, a strong force being in readiness in case the Fenians should attempt to rescue the murderers.

On the 10th of December an attempt was made by their friends to liberate some Fenians confined in Clerkenwell Prison. The police had received warning and were on the alert inside the buildings; but one of the conspirators wheeled a barrel of powder against the outside wall, lighted a fuse, and then ran away. An explosion took place; several houses near the spot were almost destroyed; twelve persons were killed or died from the effects of their injuries, 120 were wounded.

3. THE ABYSSINIAN EXPEDITION.

In 1867 an expedition was sent to Abyssinia, a country in Africa ruled over by a savage monarch named Theodore. Unfortunately, owing to the carelessness of certain officials, a letter which he sent to the Queen remained unanswered, and out of spite he seized and kept prisoners Captain Cameron, our consul, and some other Europeans residing in the country. Nothing was done for the rescue of these prisoners until the Conservatives came into power; an expedition was then organized, and the command was given to Sir Robert Napier.

Horses, cattle, camels, and mules were purchased in immense numbers, and in September a pioneer force of 1500 men sailed from India and landed in Annesley Bay, the nearest point on the Red Sea to Abyssinia. In December the main body of the expedition arrived there.

The landing-place was a mere desert of sand; everything had to be done, piers made, storehouses erected, and, most important of all, water to be obtained. The latter was the main difficulty; the nearest wells were twelve miles away, and these afforded water only for a few animals, and there were in all some 24,000 transport animals landed at Annesley Bay.

The steamers which conveyed the troops and stores were all set to work condensing fresh water from the sea-water, but the supplies were altogether insufficient, and many thousands of camels died of thirst. The pioneer party had before the arrival of the main body pushed up a terrible ravine known as the Sooroo Pass to the Plateau of Senafe, 6000 feet above the sea, and some 50 miles away. Bodies of men had been for some time at work clearing away the massive boulders which in many places blocked the ravines, and in forming a road practicable for animals.

The first half of the journey of the troops lay through the dominions of the King of Tigre, who was friendly to us; that is to say, he was glad at the advent of an expedition which would, he hoped, break the power of his dreaded neighbour. The country, although naturally fertile, was thinly populated, only two towns of any size being passed on the way. The expedition excited the greatest interest among the natives, who were astonished at everything they saw, but especially at the elephants that carried the mountain battery of guns.   Elephants are found in Abyssinia, but are regarded with the greatest dread by the natives, and the fact that we should have trained and made useful this terrible beast gave them a very high idea of the power of the white man.

Nevertheless they did not believe that we seriously intended to fight Theodore.   In Abyssinia the priests only wore anything on their heads, and in their eyes the white helmets of the soldiers gave them an eminently peaceful appearance.   As to the muskets that they carried, the natives firmly believed that they were intended as a present for Theodore.   During the last half of the march the country was difficult, and there were many places where even undisciplined troops might have offered a very formidable resistance; but Theodore, instead of defending these points, had retired with his army and a great portion of his people to the hill fortress of Magdala, which he believed to be absolutely impregnable.

4. THE CAPTURE OF MAGDALA.

When the army arrived within sight of this position Theodore sent out his army to attack the advance guard. The natives fought valiantly, but had no chance whatever with our troops, whose fire inflicted terrible loss upon them, and they were defeated without a single man having been killed on our side.   The greater part of them fled across the country and did not return to the fortress, but those who did so carried such tales of the power of the English guns that the rest determined to fight no more.   Theodore now sent in the captives, hoping that we should be satisfied and retire; but the general

sent back to say that he must surrender, and that if he
did so his life would be spared.   Upon the following

Magdala, from below Islamgie.

day the troops mounted on to the first plateau in front
of Magdala.   Here vast crowds of men, women, and

children were assembled; they offered no resistance, and the men being disarmed they were allowed to depart to their villages.

The troops then advanced against the fortress itself, their passions being aroused as they went by the discovery of the bodies of some four or five hundred unfortunate captives whom Theodore had massacred two days before. The fortress was held only by a score or so of men who remained faithful to Theodore to the end. Their resistance was speedily overpowered, and when the troops made their way in they found the body of Theodore lying a short distance from the gate. He was killed by a ball which entered the mouth and passed out at the back of the head; whether it was a chance shot from one of our soldiers, or whether Theodore had killed himself rather than fall into our hands, was never satisfactorily settled. This was on April 13th, 1868.

Two days afterwards the houses in Magdala were all burned, and the expedition returned to the sea, having satisfactorily attained the object for which they had been sent. The little son of Theodore was brought to England, and was carefully brought up and educated at the expense of government.

In Parliament Mr. Gladstone brought forward a resolution in favour of the disestablishment of the Church of Ireland, a measure which he considered would give satisfaction to the Irish and restore good feeling between the two nations. Unfortunately these expectations have not been in any way fulfilled; but the resolution was largely supported in the house, government was defeated, and in the autumn Mr. Gladstone became prime-minister instead of Mr. Disraeli.

Chapter XX.—THE PRINCE OF WALES' ILLNESS.

1. THE QUEEN'S BOOK.

Great indignation was excited in England in the course of the spring of 1868 by an attempt to assassinate the Duke of Edinburgh in Australia. The assailant, O'Farrell, an Irish Fenian, fired a pistol at him from behind and wounded him in the back; fortunately the wound was not fatal. On the 13th of May the Queen laid the foundation stone of the new buildings for St. Thomas's Hospital on the banks of the Thames facing the House of Commons, and on the 20th of June held a review of 27,000 volunteers in Windsor Park.

In August she went abroad and spent a month in Switzerland. About the same time the Queen's book, *Leaves from the Journal of our Life in the Highlands from 1841 to 1861*, made its appearance. The object of the publication of her Journals by the Queen was the same as that of her *Early Life of the Prince Consort*, namely, to show to her subjects her late husband in his character of a husband and a father. The two volumes effected the object which the Queen desired, and increased the affection with which the memory of the Prince Consort is held throughout the country. Men had already marked and noted the wisdom with which he conducted himself in his difficult position and were aware of his unwearied exertions in the cause of science and art, and for the benefit of the working-classes: they were now made familiar with his private life, as one of the most tender and loving of husbands, as one of the most affectionate and judicious of fathers.

2. THE EDUCATION ACT.

In 1869 Mr. Gladstone passed through Parliament the bill for the Disestablishment of the Irish Church. The year was not marked by any prominent event in the life of the Queen, except that in November she opened the new Thames bridge at Blackfriars and the Holborn Viaduct, London.

The year 1870 was a quiet one in England. But a bill of the highest importance was passed through Parliament this year, being brought in by Mr. Forster. Its object was to secure efficient school provision in every district of England. Up to that time all schools had been provided by voluntary effort, and although an immense deal had been done this way, the schools were wholly insufficient to contain the children of this country. It was therefore proposed that wherever the school accommodation was insufficient, school-boards, elected by the ratepayers, should have power to build sufficient schools; and furthermore, all parents were to be compelled to send their children to school.

The bill was received with general satisfaction in the house; but although brought in by the Liberal government, many of its provisions were strongly opposed by ordinary supporters of the ministry, while Mr. Forster received the support of the Conservatives. The bill was carried in the Commons by an immense majority, and passed through the Lords without opposition. The result has been excellent. Multitudes of schools have sprung up as if by magic, and, with a few exceptions, the whole of the children of this country are at present receiving education.

But while in England the year 1870 was passing quietly, on the Continent a mighty war had broken out between France and Germany. The former was com-

Scene from the Franco-German War.

pletely defeated, and the emperor was himself made prisoner at the disastrous battle of Sedan.

An insurrection broke out in Paris when the news arrived, a republic was proclaimed, the empress fled in disguise, reached a seaport, and was carried in an English gentleman's yacht to England, where she was afterwards joined by the emperor. The German army marched on to Paris and besieged that town; they defeated the various armies which the French raised to relieve the

capital, and Paris was at last forced by hunger to surrender. The King of Prussia had before this been crowned
Emperor of Germany at Versailles. Peace was at last
made on the terms of France surrendering the province
of Alsace and part of Lorraine to Germany, and paying
a very large sum of money as an indemnity.

3. THE PRINCE'S ILLNESS.

In 1871 an event occurred which filled the Queen and
her people with anxiety. The Prince of Wales had been
spending a few days at the seat of Lord Londesborough
near Scarborough, and there had, probably from the
effect of bad drainage, become very unwell. Several
other persons who had been staying in the house were
also attacked by symptoms of typhoid fever, and one of
them, the Earl of Chesterfield, died.

The prince's illness did not become serious until after
he returned to Sandringham, his seat in Norfolk. The
illness then rapidly assumed a more serious character, and
became precisely similar to that which had proved fatal
to his father. As soon as it was known that the illness
was a dangerous one the greatest anxiety was shown
by the whole nation, and the warmest sympathy was
manifested for the Queen and Princess of Wales. In
every town and village throughout the country the
reports issued twice a day by the doctors were looked for
with an anxiety as great as if the prince had been a
member of each family there. Throughout the British
colonies the same anxiety existed.

For several days the prince remained in a state of
extreme danger, and at one time hope was all but abandoned. Prayers were offered up in all the churches

of the United Kingdom, and at last, cn the 14th of December, the anniversary of the death of the Prince Consort, the telegraph flashed the news over the country that there was a slight change for the better. The corner once turned, the improvement was rapid, and on the 18th the Queen, who with most of the members of the royal family had for some time been at Sandringham, was able to leave with the assurance that the danger was past.

On the 26th the Queen wrote a letter in which she warmly expressed her deep sense of the sympathy shown by the people towards both herself and the Princess of Wales during those painful and terrible days, as well as of the general joy at the improvement in the Prince of Wales' state. These manifestations of sympathy, she wrote, " have made a deep and lasting impression on her heart, which can never be effaced. It was, indeed, nothing new to her, for the Queen had met with the same sympathy when, just ten years ago, a similar illness removed from her side the mainstay of her life, the best, wisest, and kindest of husbands. The Queen wishes to express at the same time, on the part of the Princess of Wales, her feelings of heartfelt gratitude, for she has been as deeply touched as the Queen by the great and universal manifestation of loyalty and sympathy. The Queen cannot conclude without expressing the hope that her faithful subjects will continue their prayers to God for the complete recovery of her dear son to health and strength."

As soon as the prince was sufficiently restored to take part in the ceremony a solemn thanksgiving service was held at St. Paul's, and was attended by the Queen, the prince, and the rest of the royal family. An enormous crowd lined the streets along which the procession passed, and the enthusiasm was as great as upon the occasion of the prince's entry into London with his bride. In the evening all London was illuminated, tremendous crowds filled the streets, and the feeling of sympathy and loyalty was universal throughout the whole country.

4. ROYAL MARRIAGES.

Another and more joyful event in the royal family signalized the year 1871—namely, the marriage of the Princess Louise to the Marquis of Lorne, the eldest son of the Duke of Argyll. The marriage was celebrated in St. George's Chapel, Windsor.

In February the Queen had been the subject of another attack, although this time the attempt was not a serious one. She was returning from a drive, when a lad rushed forward, holding a pistol in his right hand and a paper in his left. He was speedily seized, and the pistol proved to be unloaded; the paper which he held out was a petition for the release of the Fenian prisoners. He turned out to be an Irish lad named Arthur O'Connor, seventeen years of age, and he was afterwards tried, and sentenced to a year's imprisonment with hard labour and a flogging.

On the 1st of July the Queen paid a visit to the National Memorial, erected in Hyde Park to the memory of the Prince Consort, and two months later received the news of the death of her half-sister Feodore, who had died at Baden-Baden. At the beginning of 1873 the Emperor Napoleon died at Chislehurst.

On the 28th of May one of the Queen's grandsons,

Prince Frederick William, the son of Princess Alice of Hesse, died from the effects of an accident. He with a brother and a baby sister were in the princess's bed-room; his brother ran into an adjoining room, and the princess, knowing the window there to be open, at once went in to fetch him back; but before her return, Prince Frederick William made his way to the open window of the bed-room, and, stooping over, fell a distance of twenty feet to the ground. He died a few hours afterwards.

At the beginning of the year 1874 a general election was held, the Conservatives were returned by a majority of fifty, and Mr. Disraeli came into office as prime-minister in place of Mr. Gladstone.

In January, 1874, another royal marriage, which, however, was not celebrated in England, took place, the Duke of Edinburgh marrying the Grand Duchess Marie, daughter of the Czar of Russia. The marriage ceremony was performed in the Winter Palace at St. Petersburg. In March the prince and his bride made a public entry into London, and although a heavy snow-storm took place at the time, a great crowd assembled, and heartily cheered the newly-married pair, as, accompanied by the Queen and Princess Beatrice, they drove through the streets.

CHAPTER XXI.—THE ASHANTI EXPEDITION.

1. THE CAUSE OF THE WAR.

Beyond the boundary of the territory under British protection around the colony of the Gold Coast, in western Africa, lived the Ashantis, a savage and bar-

barous tribe, continually at war with their neighbours. In 1873 they crossed the river Prah, which formed the frontier line, and invaded the colony, their pretext being that they had certain rights of possession over Elmina, a town we had just taken over from the Dutch. They easily defeated our native allies, and advanced towards the coast.

The inhabitants of the native town of Elmina revolted; and on the refusal of the chiefs to give up their arms, the place was bombarded and set on fire by the British ships of war on the station. Two or three thousand Ashantis now advanced against Elmina, but they were gallantly attacked and driven off by a small British force, consisting partly of marines and sailors, and aided by a body of Houssas, a warlike tribe, some of whom we had enlisted in our service.

Sir Garnet Wolseley, with a large staff of officers, was now sent out to see if the Fantis—one of the friendly tribes—could not be organized and made available, so as to avoid the necessity of sending British troops to such an unhealthy climate.

Just as Sir Garnet Wolseley left England, Commodore Commerell, who had arrived in the *Rattlesnake* from the Cape of Good Hope, made a boat expedition up the Prah. They had gone but a short distance when the enemy opened such a heavy fire upon them from the bush that four men were killed and sixteen wounded, among the latter being the commodore himself. Sir Garnet Wolseley, on his arrival, was not long in finding that the attempt to form an army of Fantis was hopeless, and he wrote home requesting that the regiments he had selected might be immediately sent out. Two useful

(399) L

regiments of Fantis were, however, raised and drilled by the English officers.

Several unimportant fights now took place with the Ashantis, the latter being always defeated with considerable loss. The most serious fighting was at one of our advance posts garrisoned by the black regiment commanded by Major Russell, but he repulsed the attacks with a heavy loss, and maintained himself until Sir Garnet Wolseley arrived with assistance from Cape Coast Castle. The Ashantis lost heart and retreated across the Prah, and thus before the arrival of the troops from England the British protectorate was cleared of the invaders.

2. THE ADVANCE UP COUNTRY.

Preparations were now made for the advance, Coomassie, the Ashanti capital, being the goal of the expedition. A road was cleared through the forest which covered the whole country as far as the Prah, and huts were erected for the use of the troops. Stores were collected on the river, and all was in readiness by the 1st of January, 1874, when the troops arrived from England. Another expedition under the command of Captain Glover, R.N., an officer of much experience on the coast, was also to co-operate with that of Sir Garnet Wolseley. Captain Glover had, with the assistance of a few English officers, raised a large native force at the mouth of the river Volta, and moved forward at the same time as the expedition from Cape Coast Castle. But as he had much further to march he did not reach Coomassie until after it had been destroyed, although he rendered good service in distracting the attention of the enemy, who were obliged to divide their forces to oppose the two advancing columns.

The main difficulty of the expedition was the want of transport. The climate is so unhealthy that horses will not live there, and everything had to be carried upon the heads of the natives. The management of this matter was the chief difficulty of the expedition, for so timid were the natives that even good payment could not tempt sufficient numbers to engage in the work, and at last it was necessary absolutely to compel them to do so. Once upon the move the expedition advanced rapidly. It consisted of the 42d Highlanders, the Rifle Brigade, 200 men of the 23d Fusiliers, 350 men of the 2d West Indian regiment, a naval brigade, and Wood and Russell's native regiments.

After a short stay on the Prah, while the bridge across the river was being built, the troops crossed this stream and advanced; but the climate was already doing its work, and out of 1800 Europeans, 215 were already unfit for duty. As they advanced the king became evidently alarmed, and sent in two German missionaries and a French trader, whom he had for some months kept prisoners. He also sent letters saying he wanted peace, but as he did not forward the hostages which were demanded, the army continued its advance.

3. THE CAPTURE OF COOMASSIE.

As the column advanced information was obtained that the enemy were in force near the village of Amoaful, and the troops prepared for the attack. The nature of the ground was altogether in favour of irregular fighting. The whole country was covered thickly with lofty trees, while below was a thick underwood, through which the pioneers had to cut their way before the troops could advance. The scouts under Lord Gifford led the way, the English infantry moved in the centre, while Wood and Russell's regiments, with the naval brigade divided between them, were on the right and left flanks.

The scouts were soon engaged, and the 42d Highlanders, moving up to their assistance, were quickly in action, and on all sides the roar of fire broke out. Not content with trying to check our advance, the Ashantis made desperate efforts to retake a village which we had taken at the first rush, and for three hours little progress was made. The extreme thickness of the wood rendered it almost impossible for the three columns to advance abreast as had been intended, and every foot of the way had to be cut by the pioneers in front of the columns. While engaged on this work a great number of the troops were wounded. For the most part, however, the wounds were not serious, the Ashantis using slugs, that is, pieces of lead roughly chopped up, instead of bullets.

Gradually we won our way, but it was not until some companies of the rifles pushed forward to the assistance of the Highlanders that the Ashantis were forced back. So well did they fight, however, that just when it was supposed that the battle was at an end, they swept round and attacked us in rear, and for an hour the fight was as severe as it had been at first. The battle lasted altogether twelve hours, extending along two and a half miles of the road. At the end of that time the enemy drew off, and Amoaful was occupied.

The expedition advanced to the river Ordah, some ten miles from Coomassie, behind which point the Ashantis had gathered 10,000 strong to oppose us. By the next morning the Royal Engineers, after working all night in a heavy storm of wind and rain, had completed the bridge. The Rifle Brigade were this time in front, and no sooner had they crossed the bridge than the fighting began. Steadily the troops pushed on until they reached a village, a mile from the river. Then they lay down on each side of the path and kept back the Ashantis, while the carriers with the provisions, hammocks, and hospital appliances passed through.

A halt took place at the village. The troops lined the clearing round it, and repulsed the continued attacks of the Ashantis, and at noon the advance recommenced. Again and again the enemy tried to check our progress, but they were steadily driven back. Village after village was won, until the whole Ashanti army broke and fled towards Coomassie. The troops, after another halt, pushed on, passed the great swamp which surrounds the town without opposition, and entered Coomassie. Three cheers were given for the Queen. It was found that the king, and all the persons of distinction, had fled, and as he would not return, and the health of the troops was becoming seriously impaired, Coomassie and the royal palace were burned, and the expedition marched back again to the coast.

4. MR. PLIMSOLL AND THE SAILORS.

The first session of the Disraeli ministry (1874) was a quiet one. The most interesting feature of the year was the discussion of a measure to protect sailors from being sent to sea in vessels unfit for the voyage. This was introduced by Mr. Plimsoll. Mr. Plimsoll's attention had for some time been turned to the condition of our merchant seamen, and he found that the state of the law left them almost entirely at the mercy of such ship-owners as cared for nothing but money. A vessel could be insured for over her value, and it therefore mattered little to the ship-owner whether she went to the bottom or not. It was a well-known fact that many vessels went to sea in a positively dangerous condition, and there was little doubt that many of the wrecks that took place were due to these causes.

Mr. Plimsoll began his crusade against ship-owners by publishing a book called *Our Seamen: An Appeal*, which created a great sensation. The bill which he brought in was rejected by a majority of only three, and the following year government introduced a Merchant Shipping Bill of their own. The press of business, however, prevented it from being pushed, and it was withdrawn towards the end of July. In his disappointment and anger at this Mr. Plimsoll lost all self-control. He rose in his place, denounced some of the ship-owners in the house, and called them villains who had sent brave men to death.

When interrupted by the Speaker he repeated again and again that they were villains, and that he would abide by his words, and he then rushed out of the house in a state of wild excitement. A week afterwards Mr. Plimsoll appeared in the House of Commons and made a full apology for the language he had used, but the effect of his outburst was great in the country. It was undeniable that in his eagerness for the cause he had taken up he had listened too much to interested people; that he had brought charges against individuals which were wholly unjust; and that in many cases his statements were exaggerated and erroneous; and yet it was felt that he was, in the main, right.

Men admired the ardour and devotion which he displayed on behalf of the sailors, and public meetings were held in many parts of the country, and resolutions passed, that the law should be altered, and that protection should be given to our sailors. Public feeling was indeed so strong that finally a Merchant Shipping Bill was brought in and passed, carrying out many of the reforms which Mr. Plimsoll had advocated. The principal of these was the painting of a line on the side of every ship to show how deeply she could be loaded with safety, and no vessel laden beyond this point is now allowed to go to sea.

This mark is known as the "Plimsoll line," and the adoption of the regulation has undoubtedly saved a large number of lives since it was first instituted. Several proposals have since been made for preventing the insurance of vessels beyond two-thirds or three-quarters of their value, so as to give ship-owners a strong motive for doing all that they can towards making their vessels sea-worthy, but the subject is so difficult that it has not as yet been settled.

Chapter XXII.—THE AFGHAN WAR.

1. THE PRINCE OF WALES IN INDIA.

The Queen had intended to open Parliament at the commencement of 1875, but an alarming illness of Prince Leopold prevented her from doing so. The prince from his childhood had never been strong, and this was the third time that he had been brought to death's door from illness. He recovered, and for some years it was hoped that he had outgrown the weakness of constitution which he had hitherto manifested.

In August as the Queen was crossing from Osborne to Gosport in the royal yacht *Albert*, the steamer came in collision with the yacht *Mistletoe*, belonging to Mr. Heywood of Manchester. The *Mistletoe* sank immediately; a sister-in-law of the owner was drowned, and the captain so injured by a spar that he died.

In October the Prince of Wales started for a tour through India. Landing at Bombay he visited the military station at Poona and the native court at Baroda. He then went down by ship to Ceylon, and thence landed on the mainland and took the train to Madras, stopping at Madura and Trinchinopoli. Then he proceeded by ship to Calcutta, and thence up the country, visiting all the principal towns of India. He also paid visits to several of the great native princes.

Everywhere he was received with the greatest enthusiasm, and the scenes presented during his route were wonderful, both in the brilliancy of colour and the variety and picturesque nature of the decorations. The cities vied with each other in the effort they made to testify their loyalty to the heir to the throne. The roads were lined with dense masses of people in their picturesque attire; every house was decorated with flags and banners; triumphal arches, many of them of the most gorgeous description, were everywhere erected. The processions, comprising great numbers of elephants carrying the native chiefs, and with trappings and decorations of the greatest splendour, paraded the streets.

Native troops in every variety of costume, camels with artillery, ladies in howdahs on elephants, bands of strange barbaric music, defiled in countless numbers before the prince. There were magnificent balls and entertainments in all the chief cities; great reviews were held of British and native troops, and hunting parties on an extensive scale were organized. From end to end the journey was

Elephant with Howdah.

a panorama of magnificence, and it would have been impossible to have exceeded the cordiality and loyalty of the welcome which the prince everywhere received.

At the beginning of 1876 Mr. Disraeli announced to Parliament that the title of her Majesty would be altered, and that she would henceforth be called the Empress of India, as well as Queen of Great Britain and Ireland.

The proposal met at first with lively opposition in the house; but it was finally settled, and the appropriateness of the title has long been recognized by the public. In August Mr. Disraeli was made Earl of Beaconsfield by the Queen.

2. THE WAR IN TURKEY.

But although all was quiet in England, serious disturbances had commenced in the East. An insurrection, fostered by Russia, broke out in Bulgaria, a part of European Turkey. Instead of sending regular troops to suppress it, the Turkish government called out the local irregulars. These speedily suppressed the insurrection, but, in so doing, committed horrible atrocities. Vast numbers of Russian officers now passed over into Servia, and that country and Montenegro, in which Russian influence had always been supreme, declared war against Turkey. The Montenegrins, a hardy race of mountaineers, fought with great bravery and kept the Turks at bay. The Servians, on the contrary, in spite of the efforts of their Russian officers, were unable to make any effectual stand against the Turks, who, had they been left to themselves, would very speedily have crushed down all opposition. Russia, however, intervened to save Servia, and insisted upon an armistice. A conference of the ambassadors of all the powers was held in Constantinople, but it accomplished nothing, and in April, 1877, Russia declared war against Turkey. Two months later, a Russian army crossed the Danube.

The Turks made a gallant resistance. Osman Pasha threw up works at Plevna, and repulsed all the Russian attacks with tremendous slaughter. Russia, indeed, was making no way, although both Servia and Montenegro had joined her, until Roumania also joined the alliance, and, sending a small but well-appointed army to aid the Russians, turned the scale. The Turks were now gradually overpowered; their soldiers fought with the greatest gallantry, but their generals were wholly incompetent. The Russians advanced, carried, after severe fighting, the passes of the Balkans, and moved on against Constantinople.

The progress of the Russian arms towards this capital was viewed with alarm in England, and Lord Beaconsfield took steps to secure its safety. An English fleet sailed up to Constantinople, Indian troops were brought to the Mediterranean, and every preparation was made for the landing of an English army to defend the Turkish capital. Russia, seeing that England was determined to fight rather than allow her to occupy Constantinople, now made peace. A congress was held at Berlin in 1878, and the terms of the treaty arranged, Bulgaria being made into a virtually independent country.

In September, 1876, the Queen presented new colours to the 79th Regiment, of which the Duke of Kent, her father, had been colonel. She opened Parliament in 1877, and at the end of that year paid a visit to Lord Beaconsfield, to whom she was personally greatly attached, at his residence, Hughenden, near High Wycombe, in Buckinghamshire. In the following year she held a review of the fleet at Spithead.

At the end of 1878 the Queen suffered a very severe blow in the death of her daughter the Princess Alice of Hesse. Diphtheria had broken out in the royal palace at Darmstadt, and the royal children were attacked.

One of them, the Princess Marie, died on the 16th of November. The princess nursed her children with the greatest devotion, having them constantly in her arms, and the result was that she too caught the infection, and on the 14th of December, the anniversary of her father's death, she passed away. The deep sorrow which the Queen and royal family felt at the death of the princess was shared in both by the people of Great Britain and those of Hesse. At home she had always been very popular, and her devotion to the Queen and the noble way in which she had been her mother's support and comfort on the occasion of the death of the Prince Consort, had specially endeared her to the people.

In March, 1879, the Duke of Connaught was married to Princess Louise of Prussia, and on the 12th of May the Queen's first great-grandchild, the daughter of Princess Charlotte of Prussia, who had the year before married the Prince of Saxe-Meiningen, was born.

3. THE INVASION OF AFGHANISTAN.

For many years the relations between ourselves and Afghanistan had been unsatisfactory. Shere Ali, the Afghan ruler, received an annual subsidy from us, and had been presented with large quantities of arms. He became alarmed by the approach of Russia towards his northern frontier, and being unable to obtain assurances from us that we would protect him from Russia, he determined to throw himself into the hands of that power. He had long refused to allow any British officer to go to Cabul; but, from a native source, it was known that a Russian general with an escort had been received there by the ameer with great honour.

The Viceroy of India thereupon wrote to the ameer to request him to receive a British mission. The ameer gave no decisive answer, and Major Cavagnari, an officer of great experience in Afghanistan, was sent forward to inform the ameer that an important mission was about to start. He was, however, stopped by a strong Afghan force a few miles after crossing the frontier, and forced to return. It was impossible for Britain to submit to see Russian envoys received by a country on her border which refused to admit a mission from her, and preparations were at once made for war. This was about the middle of 1878.

It was decided to invade Afghanistan with three columns. A letter was sent to the ameer saying that the army would cross the frontier unless an answer was received from him by the 20th of November granting our demands. No answer came, and the next day two of the columns crossed the frontier. One of these, under the command of General Sir S. Browne, advanced up the Khyber Pass. In addition to the main force advancing along the valley, two columns were sent out by General Browne to make a detour through the mountains and to come down behind the Afghan position at Ali Musjid.

As soon as the main column was seen from this fort the guns opened fire. The men had been practising for some weeks and had got the range accurately, and the shot fell thick and fast. The column was therefore halted, as it was considered advisable that the flanking columns should have time to make their long detour before the attack was made. A battery of heavy guns drawn by elephants was brought up and opened fire with great effect upon the fort. The infantry now mounted the slopes on both sides and the fight between them and the Afghans who were swarming there soon became very animated.

The hillsides from top to bottom were dotted with tiny puffs of musketry, while from the fortress and from the English batteries in the valley the roar of the heavy cannon was almost incessant.   Our infantry had won

Fort of Ali Musjid in the Khyber Pass.

their way along the hillsides until they were abreast of the forts, but the Afghan intrenchments were here very strong and an attack could not be made without great loss of life, therefore it was determined to halt on the ground we had won until morning.

In the course of the night the two flanking columns, which had met with enormous difficulties on the way, arrived at their destination.   The Afghans were seized with a panic on learning that British troops were coming down into the valley behind them; and, abandoning the fort and all their strong positions, fled in the greatest haste. The column now moved on up the valley to Jellalabad without meeting with any resistance.

4. THE SECOND MASSACRE AT CABUL.

The second main column, under the command of General Roberts, entered the Kuram Valley, and, after four days' march, found the Afghans occupying a strong position on the crest of a hill known as the Peiwar Kotal. The position was too strong to be carried by a front attack, but by a long night march the troops reached the crest of the hill on the Afghan left without being observed. The Afghans then flocked out to the attack, and there was fierce fighting for some hours, but General Roberts moved his troops as if to threaten the rear of the Afghans, and these, on seeing their line of retreat threatened, at once abandoned their position, and fled precipitately over the mountains to Cabul. As the pass by which they had retreated was soon afterwards closed by snow, there was no fear of their returning to take the offensive, and after some fighting with the natives of the valleys, the force settled down into winter quarters.

The third main column, under General Stewart, entered Afghanistan by the Bolan Pass, and marched to Candahar without encountering any serious resistance.

On the arrival of the fugitives from his armies in the Khyber Pass and the Kuram Valley, the ameer fled from his capital to take refuge with his friends the Russians, but his disappointment at the destruction of his hopes broke him down, and he died on the way. He was succeeded by his son Yakoob Khan, who had been kept by him for many years in captivity. The new ameer at once opened negotiations with us, came down to the British camp and had an interview with Sir S. Browne, and a treaty of peace was concluded between them.

In accordance with the terms of the treaty, and by a special invitation of the ameer, a mission proceeded to Cabul. It consisted of Sir Louis Cavagnari, for that officer had recently received the honour of knighthood, two officers, a surgeon, twenty-five native cavalry, and fifty native infantry. They were well received at Cabul, the ameer treated them with cordiality and friendliness, and all went well till the arrival in the city of some regiments from Herat. These troops had taken no part in the fighting against the British, consequently their belief in their own power was as great as ever, and they were loud in their complaints that peace should have been made with us before they had been brought up to try their strength with us.

The friendly spirit with which the mission had at first been received was speedily changed after the arrival of the regiments from Herat. The men were threatened and cursed as they walked in the streets, and the situation became alarming. The ameer was appealed to, and he assured the mission that there was no danger, that his protection would be sufficient for them, and that the Cabul troops would at once, at his orders, put down the Herati men should they show signs of insubordination. There is little doubt, however, that Yakoob was perfectly aware of what was being prepared, and that he was a party to the attack on the mission. At anyrate, during the whole time it was going on he sat in his palace close by, and took no step whatever either to call off the troops or to order up the Cabul regiments.

Sir Louis Cavagnari was well aware of the danger, but determined to remain at his post and do his duty. He was told by an officer of one of our native regiments, who was an Afghan born, and was spending his leave in his native village near Cabul, that there was great danger of a rising by the Heratis, and the massacre of the white officers. To this he replied quietly, "They can only kill the three or four of us who are here, and our deaths will be avenged by our country." On the night of the 2d of September, 1879, the Herati troops, aided by the rabble of the town, attacked the mission, the members of which were lodged in a wooden building close to the palace of Yakoob. The native cavalry escort were away out on the plain, and there were only the fifty infantry available for the defence.

They belonged to the corps of guides, which is raised among the hill tribes, and were therefore kindred in blood and religion to the assailants of the mission, who shouted to them to come out and join them; but the men were true to their officers, and defended the place with the greatest gallantry. For many hours the little band, with its four British officers, resisted the attack of many thousands of the enemy, hoping always that the Cabul regiments would be brought up to their rescue; but although the ameer was urged by his wisest and most trusted counsellors to take this step, he refused to do so, but sat silent and sullen all night, while the struggle was going on just outside his palace.

At last the Afghans, finding that they could not overcome the resistance of the defenders of the house, brought up cannon, and opened fire upon it. Still the defence was maintained, until at last the house was set on fire by the enemy's shells. Then the few survivors of the band burst out, and died fighting to the last in the midst of countless foes.

Chapter XXIII.—THE AFGHAN WAR No. II.

1. THE OCCUPATION OF CABUL.

No sooner did the news of the atrocious massacre reach India than the troops were again set in motion. Those in the Kuram Valley prepared at once to advance, and as soon as a few more troops arrived from India the force moved forward under the command of General Roberts. When they had advanced two days' march towards Cabul, the ameer, accompanied by some of his principal nobles, rode into camp. He declared that he was unable to control the people, and that he had come in to show his friendship to the English; but he was received with coldness, and was virtually treated as a prisoner. There were indeed very strong grounds for suspecting him of treachery, as he had made no effort whatever to save the mission, who had gone to Cabul not only in accordance with the terms of the treaty, but at his special invitation, and on the assurance of his protection.

Great crowds of the hill tribes gathered round the column in readiness to pour down and repeat the former massacre of Cabul, should an opportunity offer; but they abstained from an attack until, as they expected, our troops should be beaten when they reached a strong position occupied by thirteen Afghan regiments, with numerous artillery, on the hills a few miles from Cabul. General Roberts had only half his troops with him, the rest being occupied in guarding and bringing up the baggage a day's march in the rear. No time was to be

General Roberts

lost, however, for the attitude of the tribesmen swarming round was so defiant that, should hesitation in attacking the Afghan position be shown, the whole host of enemies would doubtless pour down upon us.

Confiding in the valour of his troops, he therefore ordered them to attack at once. Furious at the treacherous massacre of their comrades at Cabul, the soldiers advanced with ardour to the attack; and the Afghans, astonished at seeing them press onward, without pause or hesitation, through the fire kept up upon them, became irresolute, hesitated, then gave way, and were soon in full flight towards Cabul. As our cavalry were in the rear of the column, they could not be brought up in time to overtake the fugitives before these gained the cover of some large villages out on the plain.

The Herati regiments had, however, had enough of fighting, and the next morning it was found that they had all marched away, and that Cabul was open to us. The army marched forward and took possession of the city, capturing the ameer's walled camp at Sherpur, where seventy-five guns were taken. The ameer's palace in the fort, called the Bala Hissar, on the hill above the town, was occupied by the troops; but a serious misfortune took place here. Large quantities of powder were found stored in various buildings, and either by accident or by the work of the natives, two great explosions took place. Fortunately only twelve of our men were killed.

The ameer now resigned, and, as there was no actual evidence that he had been a party to the attack upon the mission, he was not tried for that crime, but was sent into India, and there detained in secure captivity. As soon as winter closed the passes, and cut off the force at Cabul from India, the Afghans assembled in vast numbers. Ten thousand men encountered a little body of about 220 British cavalry, with four light guns. The enemy at once attacked, and, unchecked by the fire of the guns, streamed down upon them. The little body of cavalry charged straight at the advancing masses, in order to give the artillerymen time to draw off the guns.

They fought their way into the midst of the enemy's infantry, but their progress was at last arrested by sheer weight of numbers. They turned and cut their way out again, with great loss in killed and wounded. The country was cut up with dikes and water-courses, across which the guns could not be dragged as fast as the enemy followed. Traces were therefore cut, and the guns were for a time abandoned. The enemy then advanced towards Cabul, but their progress was checked by 200 Highlanders, and this gave time for the other troops to get under arms, and for two columns, which had been out scouring the country, to return.

2. A NATIVE RISING.

Although for the moment the advance of the Afghans upon Cabul had been arrested, this was but temporary, for masses were pouring down into the plain from all the surrounding hills and valleys, until at last 25,000 men were threatening the British force. Five or six thousand occupied a position on the hills above the town. After two days' severe fighting these were driven off, while our cavalry, charging the masses in the plains, prevented them from advancing upon the town. The next day another effort was made to clear the hills, and this, after hard fighting, succeeded. But no sooner had the British gained this success than a fresh Afghan force, 20,000 strong, advanced, while from other quarters masses of the enemy approached.

General Roberts' troops then evacuated their positions, and retired to the Sherpur camp, and in spite of the 40,000 Afghans who surrounded them, the movement was completed without serious loss (Dec. 1879).

For some days they were molested by a constant fire kept up from walls and houses within reach of the encampment, and on the night of the 22d Dec. the enemy attacked in immense force. But information had been received of their intention; the troops were in readiness, and received them with such a tremendous fire that the Afghans paused, and could not bring up their courage to the point of making a rush against the position so stoutly held. At daybreak next morning the cavalry moved out from the rear of the camp, made a circuit, and fell upon the enemy, who at once fled to the shelter of the city, numbers being cut down in their retreat.

The following day the head of a relieving force, which had been pushing forward from Jellalabad, was seen in the distance. The Afghans poured down to attack them, but the troops at Sherpur moved out to their assistance, and the Afghans, seeing that they had now no hope of success, abandoned Cabul, and fled away to their homes and villages.

In the spring General Stewart marched with his army from Candahar to join General Roberts. At Ahmed Khel he was opposed by some 15,000 tribesmen. He advanced to the attack, when down poured about 4000 Ghazis, as they were called, that is to say fanatics, sworn to give their lives to carry out their object of exterminating the hated infidels.

These men are armed, some with rifles and matchlocks, some with heavy swords, knives, and pistols; others with pikes, made with bayonets, or pieces of sharpened iron fastened to sticks. Some were on foot and some on horseback, and so rapidly did they come on that they were upon the British before the latter could prepare to receive them. Our cavalry were moving in front of the infantry, and these prevented some of our men from firing. Before they could be moved out of the way, or got in line for a charge, the Ghazis were upon them. In a moment all was smoke, dust, and confusion. The ammunition mules took fright and ran off, riderless horses dashed here and there; the Ghazis rushed in rear of our infantry, and a desperate hand-to-hand struggle took place, the enemy fighting with heroic bravery, without the slightest regard for their lives. One of the regiments thus attacked was English; another composed of Sikhs; the third of Ghoorkas. All fought with equal bravery, pouring tremendous volleys into the ranks of the enemy. So fiercely did the latter charge that they came to within thirty yards of the mouths of the guns of the artillery, which were only protected by the cavalry charging again and again in the most gallant manner. At last the Ghazis fell back, leaving a thousand dead on the field. besides those whose dead bodies they had carried off.

3. THE BATTLE OF MAIWAND.

The column again advanced. Ghuznee opened its gates without opposition, for most of the fighting men had been engaged at Ahmed Khel, and had had enough of it. The fanatics, however, again gathered, and a column was sent against them. They fought as bravely as before, but our men, being this time prepared, inflicted such heavy losses upon them that they were unable to make their way to close quarters. The resistance then ceased, and General Stewart marched on to Cabul without further fighting (May, 1880).

For some months the forces remained quiet at Cabul.

An Afghan prince named Abdulrahman had now assumed
the ameership, and had been received cordially in the
north of Afghanistan; and as the British government
were most anxious to retire from the country, his authority was recognized by us, and the British force prepared
to retire as he approached Cabul.   But at that moment
news came which showed that the work was not yet
over.   When General Stewart advanced from Candahar
he left a strong British force in that city.   An Afghan
noble named Wali Shere Ali had been appointed by us
as governor of Candahar, and had raised a native force.

In June the news came that Ayoub Khan, governor of
Herat, and brother to the late ameer, was advancing with
a great force against Candahar.   1500 British infantry,
500 cavalry, and six guns, under General Burrows,
marched out to the river Helmund, accompanied by the
Wali, with his army.   When Ayoub approached, the
whole of the Wali's troops deserted in a body and joined
him.   Ayoub advanced, and crossed the Helmund higher
up the river, and General Burrows fell back to a point
near the village of Maiwand, to bar his advance against
Candahar.   The British general had no idea of the very
large force with which the enemy were advancing.

The morning (27th July, 1880) was thick, and but little
could be seen of Ayoub's army until two of our guns in
advance came in contact with them and opened fire.   Our
force then drew up in order of battle—the 66th Regiment were on the right, the Bombay Grenadiers in the
centre, and the other native regiment, known as Jacob's
Rifles, on the left.   In addition to the six guns of the
Royal Artillery with the force were six others, which had
been captured from the Wali's mutineers.

The British position was a bad one, for hills rose on either side, and the enemy, placing five batteries on these, opened a terrible fire upon us. After two hours' fighting the ammunition for the Wali's guns became exhausted, and there now remained only the solitary British battery to answer the five batteries which were pouring down shot and shell among us. Up to this time the infantry had kept the masses of the enemy at bay, but they had already worked round into the village in our rear. Half an hour later Jacob's Rifles began to waver, and they gave way before the attack of the enemy's infantry, led by their Ghazis. They soon fell into utter confusion, and breaking into the ranks of the Grenadiers, who had until now fought steadily, broke them also.

Great masses of the enemy now poured down, and the 66th, broken into by the rush of the native troops on one side, pressed by the Ghazis on the other, and mown down by the artillery fire, began also to fall back, and in a few minutes the confusion became hopeless. The native cavalry, having suffered severely from the fire to which they had been exposed, refused to charge, and presently rode off from the field. Pressed back to the village, the troops made another desperate stand, and for a time the 66th defended the walls and inclosures, fighting nobly to the last, and so giving time for the rest of the troops to retreat.

SOMEBODY'S DARLING.

Into a ward of the whitewash'd halls,
   Where the dead and dying lay,
Wounded by bayonets, shells, and balls,
   Somebody's Darling was borne one day—

Somebody's Darling, so young and so brave,
　　Wearing yet on his pale sweet face,
Soon to be hid by the dust of the grave,
　　The lingering light of his boyhood's grace.

Matted and damp are the curls of gold,
　　Kissing the snow of that fair young brow,
Pale are the lips of delicate mould—
　　Somebody's Darling is dying now.
Back from his beautiful blue-veined brow
　　Brush all the wandering waves of gold,
Cross his hands on his bosom now,
　　Somebody's Darling is still and cold.

Kiss him once for somebody's sake,
　　Murmur a prayer soft and low;
One bright curl from its fair mates take,
　　They were somebody's pride, you know:
Somebody's hand had rested there,
　　Was it a mother's soft and white?
And have the lips of a sister fair
　　Been baptized in the waves of light?

God knows best; he has somebody's love;
　　Somebody's heart enshrined him there;
Somebody wafted his name above
　　Night and morn on the wings of prayer.
Somebody wept when he march'd away,
　　Looking so handsome, brave, and grand;
Somebody's kiss on his forehead lay,
　　Somebody clung to his parting hand.

Somebody's waiting and watching for him—
　　Yearning to hold him again to their heart;

And there he lies with his blue eyes dim,
   And the smiling childlike lips apart.
Tenderly bury the fair young dead,
   Pausing to drop on his grave a tear;
Carve on the wooden slab at his head,—
   "Somebody's Darling slumbers here."
                —*Mrs. Lacoste.*

4. THE END OF THE WAR.

When the Afghans had overwhelmed by their fire the last defenders of the village, they scattered to plunder the baggage, and for a time the retreat was continued without interruption. It was a terrible one. Fifty miles had to be passed, and no water was obtainable on the way. Along the whole line the villagers rose against the exhausted troops, and numbers perished from thirst, exhaustion, and the swords of the enemy before the survivors reached the shelter of Candahar. Ayoub's army had suffered such heavy losses in their conflict with this handful of British troops that it was some days before they resumed their march against Candahar, and when they arrived there they contented themselves with beleaguering the town, and made no serious attempt to attack it.

As soon as the news of the disaster at Maiwand reached Cabul, orders were issued that a portion of the army, instead of retiring, as had been intended, by the direct road to India, should march for Candahar. The new ameer afforded every assistance, and sent orders to the tribes along the line of march that the British force was not to be molested. He was, indeed, as anxious as we were that Ayoub Khan should be defeated, for if Ayoub had succeeded in capturing Candahar and destroying the

British force there, he would have been a formidable rival
to the throne.

General Roberts took the command of the force, which
consisted of 10,000 men, with 8000 camp-followers, and
as many transport and artillery mules and ponies. The
column marched the distance in nineteen days at the rate
of fifteen and a half miles a day, a distance easy enough
for a single regiment to perform, but a wonderful feat for
a force containing some 18,000 persons, with 8000 baggage animals marching through mountainous valleys.

As the force approached Candahar Ayoub drew off the
besieging force and established himself on some hills a
few miles north of the town. On the 1st of September
the army advanced to the attack. No attempt was made
to storm the hills themselves, the columns advancing so
as to sweep round their foot and thus arrive at Ayoub's
camp, which was pitched behind the hills. The ground
across which they had to advance was thickly scattered
with villages, and cut up in all directions with water-
courses. The villages swarmed with the enemy, who
opposed a desperate resistance to our advance, and every
foot of the ground had to be carried by hard fighting.
The whole Afghan force had now gathered to oppose us;
but their efforts were in vain, and in four hours from the
time the battle began the Afghan army was driven in
headlong flight from its position. Their camp and all it
contained was captured, together with thirty-three guns.
This brought the campaign to a close, and the whole of the
British troops then retired across the frontier into India.

Chapter XXIV.—THE ZULU WAR.

1. THE BRITISH ADVANCE.

In the South African colonies there had, during the reign of the Queen, been several petty wars. These caused a good deal of trouble, but were none of them serious. Towards the end of the year 1878, just after the conclusion of the Afghan war, troubles arose between us and the Zulus, a nation of savage warriors lying to the north of the colony of Natal. The attitude of this people had long been menacing. Their military organization was in its way perfect; every man was a soldier, their king a despot, who carried out wholesale executions as a punishment for the slightest opposition to his will. A variety of causes of dispute had arisen between us, but it was felt at last by Sir Bartle Frere, the high commissioner of South Africa, that it was impossible for things to continue in their present state, since the Zulu king could at any moment pour his army across the frontier and carry destruction into the whole colony.

It happened that our force in South Africa was larger than usual, and it was therefore considered a favourable opportunity to put an end to the standing danger to the colony. Accordingly a demand was sent to the Zulu king to the effect that he must dissolve his army. While awaiting his reply the whole of the troops were moved up to the frontier. The answer was evasive; but on the 12th of January, 1879, no further answer having been received, the column of Lord Chelmsford crossed the Tugela River. It advanced so slowly, however, that ten days later it had only reached Isandula, ten miles distant.

On the morning of the 22d Lord Chelmsford, taking with him the main body of the column, advanced to reconnoitre the country beyond, leaving six companies of the 24th Regiment, two guns, 104 men of a colonial corps, and 800 natives to guard the camp. These were further reinforced during the day by the arrival of Colonel Durnford with a mounted corps of colonial troops. In the afternoon the enemy were seen advancing. No preparations whatever had been made for defence, nor had any step been taken to occupy a high and steep hill which rose close to the camp.

2. THE MASSACRE OF ISANDULA.

The Zulus advanced in their usual formation, namely, in a great crescent. Two companies of the 24th went to meet them. The Zulus, however, were so numerous and came on with such determination that the rapid fire of the infantry scarcely checked them for a moment, and the latter were forced to fall back to camp. In the meantime the wings of the Zulu crescent had swept round and come down upon the baggage waggons at the back of the camp. Then the whole body fell upon the little force of British. So sudden and determined was the attack, so unexpected was its character, that there was scarcely time to make any preparation to meet it.

The troops stood their ground and poured a tremendous fire into the Zulus, but these with a fierce rush dashed upon them, and the combat became hand to hand. In a moment all was confusion and disorder. Some stood in groups and fought desperately back to back, others broke and fled. A few, and a few only, of the mounted colonial troops succeeded in cutting their way through the enemy and making for the river. The infantry were to a man killed. Two mounted officers, Lieutenants Melville and Coghill, cut their way through the surrounding Zulus. They rode for the river, hotly pursued. Lieutenant Melville swam his horse and got safely across, but seeing that his comrade was helpless in the river, his

Scene from the Zulu War.

horse having thrown him, he returned to aid him. The delay was fatal. The Zulus were upon them, and after a desperate resistance both officers were killed.

While the British force at Isandula was being destroyed by the enemy a fierce fight was going on at the spot where the army had crossed the river, which was called Rorke's Drift. Here a depot of provisions and stores had been formed. This was guarded by a force of some eighty men of the 24th Regiment under the command of Lieutenant Bromhead, Lieutenant Chard of the Royal Engineers being senior officer, and therefore in general command. In the afternoon the news reached them that the enemy was coming, and without a moment's loss of time the young officers set their men to work to form an intrenchment with the grain-bags and boxes, and so connect a house, used as an hospital, with the storehouse.

3. RORKE'S DRIFT AND EKOWE.

Scarcely were the preparations complete when several thousand Zulus poured across the river and advanced to the attack. The little garrison defended themselves with heroic bravery. Fortunately among the stores was a large quantity of ammunition, and they were therefore enabled to keep up an efficient fire without fear of running short. Several times the Zulus charged the breastwork and endeavoured to climb over, but each time these efforts were repulsed. The hospital, after desperate fighting, was carried and burned, but the attacks upon the storehouse were all beaten off. For twelve hours the fight continued, and then the Zulus, after losing over a thousand men, fell back.

Lord Chelmsford, returning with his column after his reconnaissance, found the camp he had left in the morning destroyed, and its defenders slain. The troops lay under arms expecting an attack all night, and in the morning marched back to Rorke's Drift.

In addition to the column under Lord Chelmsford, a second under Colonel Pearson had crossed the Tugela near its mouth. These had been attacked on the way, but had defended themselves so stoutly that the Zulus had been unable to come to close quarters. The column then marched on to Ekowe, an old missionary station, and there receiving the news of the disaster at Isandula, formed an intrenched camp which they resolved to hold as long as possible. The third column, under Colonel Wood, was attacked two days after the battle of Isandula, but having heard of that event, they were well prepared, and repulsed the enemy with much loss.

On the news of the disaster of Isandula arriving in England a great sensation was created, and the most strenuous efforts were made to send out reinforcements. Six regiments of infantry, two of cavalry, and two batteries of artillery were put on board ship within a few days after the news arrived. In the meantime a regiment which was at the Cape was at once sent round, and every available man landed from the men-of-war, for it was feared that the Zulus, flushed with their victory, would at once invade the colony. Had they done so they could have carried fire and sword from end to end of Natal; but it is probable that they were discouraged by the tremendous losses they had suffered at Isandula and Rorke's Drift. At anyrate they did not attempt to cross the river.

As soon as the first reinforcements landed a column set out to relieve the garrison of Ekowe. When the force arrived within a short distance of Ekowe the enemy were seen advancing. The troops were formed up in a hollow square. The Zulus came on in their usual formation, and first attacked the side held by the 60th Rifles. For half an hour they assailed that side, but, unable to withstand the terrible fire of the 60th, swept round to the right with the intention of attacking on that side, but were then exposed to the fire of two other regiments.

Nothing could exceed the gallantry with which the Zulus fought, and it was not until they had lost 1500 men that they abandoned the attack. The relieving column then marched on to Ekowe, drew off the garrison, and retired with them across the frontier again, for as yet things were not prepared for the invasion of Zululand.

4. KAMBULA AND ULUNDI.

On the 28th of March, the day before the column started for the relief of Ekowe, there had been some very severe fighting on the north-west frontier of Zululand. Colonel Evelyn Wood with his column, which had fallen back after the disaster at Isandula, had continued to harass the enemy with much success, and had determined to punish a noted chief of the name of Umbelini, who had made repeated attacks upon our positions. His stronghold lay far to the north, but he kept the greater part of his herds of cattle on an almost inaccessible plateau fifteen miles from his camp. Colonel Buller started on the morning of the 28th with all the cavalry attached to the column, consisting entirely of colonial troops, gained the plateau without difficulty, collected great herds of cattle, and prepared to return.

Just as they were on the point of leaving the plateau vast bodies of Zulus were seen approaching across the plains. This was a force sent by Cetewayo the Zulu king to the assistance of Umbelini. They attacked the cavalry as they were still entangled in the rugged descent, and desperate hand-to-hand fighting took place. The cavalry suffered severely, losing no less than eighty-six men and twelve officers. The rest of the force succeeded in getting away, and, although hotly pursued, reached the

camp of Colonel Wood at Kambula in safety. The following day the Zulus in great force approached the camp,
which had been strongly intrenched and put into a position of defence. Colonels Buller and Russell, with the
cavalry, went out to check the advance, but the masses

Caffre Chief of the Zulu Tribe.

of the enemy poured on without a check, and the cavalry
retired into the camp.

When the Zulus arrived within 300 yards of the intrenchments a heavy fire was opened upon them. This
checked their advance upon the camp, and they then
moved round and attacked the inclosure where the cattle
were kept. This was stoutly defended, and for three
hours a desperate fight raged round the whole circuit of
the camp. At the end of that time the enemy, having

suffered terribly from the fire of our breech-loaders, began
to fall back. The cavalry again sallied out and fell upon
them, and kept up the pursuit for seven miles. Our loss
in this engagement was very small.

A force of 15,000 men was now gathered ready for
the invasion of Zululand, but for months they were
kept inactive, and the greatest discontent prevailed
in the colony and in Britain at nothing being done
though so large a force was within four days' march of
the stronghold of the enemy. So strong was this feeling
that on the 26th of May Sir Garnet Wolseley was appointed to the chief command, and sailed from England
a few days later.

It was not until Sir Garnet Wolseley was daily expected
to arrive that the general in command made up his mind
to advance against Ulundi, Cetewayo's chief town. The
British troops were formed in a great square, and as
they approached the village they were attacked by the
Zulu army. The enemy came on with their accustomed
bravery and surrounded the square, but the tremendous
fire from our breech-loaders, aided by guns and Gatlings
placed at the corners of the square, mowed them down
with terrible slaughter. The conflict lasted but a few
minutes, at the end of which the Zulus took to flight,
and the war in Zululand was at an end. A few scattered
bands held together, but these were easily dispersed, and
the Zulus made off to their villages. A hot pursuit was
kept up after the king, and he was finally captured and
sent a prisoner to the Cape. Some time afterwards he
came to England, and was allowed to return to Zululand.
He never regained his former power, and a few months
afterwards was killed in a battle with a rival chief.

CHAPTER XXV.
THE WAR IN THE TRANSVAAL.

1. DEATH OF THE PRINCE IMPERIAL.

On the 1st of June, 1879, before the end of the Zulu war, a most lamentable occurrence took place. Among the many who had come out from England to take part in the war was the young Prince Napoleon. The prince had been educated at Woolwich Military Academy, and although naturally his early training, so different from that of English boys, and his comparative ignorance of our language, were great drawbacks to him, he came out very high in the final examination, a fact which proved that his talent must have been exceptionally good. He was a favourite with all who knew him; his manner was gentle and courteous, and yet he was full of high spirits, and ready to take part in every amusement.

After the disaster of Isandula he applied for leave to accompany the English army as a volunteer, in order to acquire a practical knowledge of military affairs. On the 1st of June the Prince Imperial started with Lieutenant Carey of the 98th, and six troopers belonging to a colonial corps, on a reconnoitring expedition. They arrived at a deserted village some ten miles from the camp, and here they rashly unsaddled their horses and rested for an hour. As they were in the act of resaddling a party of Zulus suddenly sprang out upon them. All, including the officer, leapt on their horses and rode off. The Prince Imperial, though an admirable horseman, was unable to mount his horse, and was overtaken by the Zulus within three hundred yards of the village and killed, making a vigorous resistance to the end.

His death under such circumstances caused the deepest regret in this country, and the greatest sympathy was felt for his widowed mother, the Empress Eugénie, under this crushing affliction.   His body was afterwards recovered and sent home, and was buried with great military pomp at Chislehurst.

2. HOME AFFAIRS.

The Conservative government had been a good deal shaken by the Afghan and Zulu wars.   Opinions differed as to the necessity for the former, but the general opinion was that the action of Sir Bartle Frere in declaring war against the Zulus had been hasty and uncalled-for.   The reverse of Isandula had been a mortification to the pride of the nation; and although success had at last been achieved, the long delay in bringing it about had caused impatience and disgust, while the magnificent bravery of the Zulus had excited a feeling of pity for them in their terrible reverses.   Moreover, the bill for the expense of the war was considerable, and England was at the time suffering severe distress.

Trade was extremely bad.   The manufacturing and mining districts were everywhere suffering, there had been an extremely bad harvest, and great numbers of the agricultural population were on the point of ruin. In Ireland the distress was great.   The consequence was that when, in the beginning of 1880, Parliament was dissolved, the Liberals were returned by a large majority.   Lord Beaconsfield resigned, and Mr. Gladstone again came into power.

In April of the following year the Earl of Beaconsfield died, and was buried at Hughenden. The funeral was attended by all the leading Conservatives in the country, and wreaths of flowers were sent up from almost every

Lord Beaconsfield.

town in England. Before the vault was closed the Queen and Princess Beatrice visited it, and laid flowers upon the coffin. A monument was afterwards erected in Hughenden church to Lord Beaconsfield "by his grateful and affectionate sovereign and friend, Victoria." The grief which was felt through England at the loss of this great statesman was deep and profound, and the anniversary of his death is still commemorated by the wearing of primroses by Conservatives throughout the kingdom.

On the 19th of September, 1881, Mr. Garfield, President of America, died after a lingering illness, the result of the pistol shot of an assassin. His illness was watched throughout Europe with a feeling of sympathy only exceeded by that which was felt on the occasion of the Prince of Wales' illness, and at his death the court went into mourning, an honour never before paid except in the cases of royal personages and members of the royal family.

3. THE RISING OF THE BOERS.

A few months after the Zulu war came to a conclusion, the Boers, a people of Dutch descent inhabiting a district called the Transvaal in South Africa, became very troublesome. They had gladly put themselves under our protection at the time when the Zulus were threatening their very existence, but as soon as we had destroyed the Zulu power they began to regret the loss of their independence. On 20th December, 1880, a large body of them suddenly fell upon 250 men of the 94th Regiment as they were marching with a train of waggons. Totally unprepared for attack the British were unable to defend themselves. In a few minutes 150 men were killed or wounded, and the rest taken prisoners. Several adherents of the British rule in various parts were massacred, and the whole country, with the exception of a few of the towns, was very shortly in the hands of the Boers.

On the 24th of January, 1881, General Sir George Colley, with two British regiments and a naval brigade, advanced from Newcastle, a place near the frontier. They moved slowly, and the Boers took up and intrenched a position known as Laing's Nek. The attack on the position was made by 870 infantry and 170 mounted men. They reached the top of the crest, but were then checked by a tremendous fire from the Dutch lines. As they hesitated the Dutch burst upon them, and they were driven back with a loss of 180 men. The troops retired to the position they had occupied in the morning, and were at once surrounded by the Boers.

On the 8th of February the general moved out with five companies of rifles and four guns to open the road back to Newcastle. When he reached some rising ground beyond the river Ingogo he was attacked on all sides by the Boers, and for six hours the fight raged. The enemy surrounded the position and kept up a fire from all sides. The ground was covered with boulders, and the Boers at times crept up to the position held by the British. So accurate was their shooting that our cannon could not be worked, as the men were shot down as fast as they attempted to load, every officer, gunner, and horse being killed or wounded within half an hour after the action began. About 160 men were killed or wounded before night came on, but as soon as it became dark the force left their position, and succeeded in regaining the camp before the Boers were aware that they had moved.

4. MAJUBA HILL.

Reinforcements now came up, and on the 26th General Colley, with twenty officers and 627 men, started from the camp with the intention of occupying Majuba Hill, a lofty mountain rising at the side of Laing's Nek. The march across the unknown country in the night was difficult in the extreme, but before daylight the troops gained the top of the hill. At sunrise the Boers discovered that the mountain which commanded their position was in the hands of the British, and at once swarmed out to the attack. For four hours a distant fire was kept up, but little harm was done to our men. The Boers crept up under shelter of the boulders until close to the summit, and then suddenly rushed forward. Our advanced line, taken by surprise, at once gave way, and the Boers, with shouts of triumph, dashed upon them.

A few of the troops stood steadily, but the greater proportion were seized with a panic, and the resistance offered was feeble in the extreme. In a few minutes the whole of the British force on the crest were either killed or captured. A stranger or more humiliating disaster never fell upon a British force.

Great numbers of troops were sent out at a vast expense from England, and just as these reached the front, and were preparing to advance, peace was made, the British government giving the Boers all they asked for. During all those months the various garrisons of British troops in the Transvaal had held out nobly, and repulsed every attack made upon them, one place only being forced to surrender by want of food. Taken all together, in its management, its disasters, and its conclusion, the Transvaal campaign is probably the least glorious of any in the history of this country.

Chapter XXVI.—THE WAR IN EGYPT.

1. THE RIOT AT ALEXANDRIA.

In the year 1882 the aspect of affairs in Egypt became very threatening. Ismail Pasha, the former khedive or ruler, had by his extravagance plunged the country into

debt, and had finally been forced to abdicate the throne
by France and Britain, and Tewfik, his son, appointed
khedive in his stead. A party in Egypt objected to the
change, and regarded Tewfik with dislike, as being in
their opinion too much under the thumb of Britain and
France. A hostile movement was begun in the army.
It was headed by a Colonel Arabi, an energetic man of
considerable talent. The object of the movement was,
in the first place, to obtain higher pay for the army, but
its real aim was to get rid of foreign influence in Egypt,
and to place native officials in the higher posts in the
administration, almost all of which were held by
Europeans.

The movement increased in strength, and the position
of Tewfik was menaced. Britain and France, having
large interests in Egypt, were afraid that, if a successful
revolution took place, free passage through the Suez Canal
might be interfered with. They therefore sent a fleet to
Alexandria, the great northern port of Egypt, to give a
moral support to the khedive, and to protect the European inhabitants. On the 11th of June a very serious riot
took place there. It began, in the first place, from a
quarrel between the natives and the lower class of Greeks,
Italians, and Maltese. The riot spread, and a considerable
number of Europeans were killed or wounded.

Britain at once prepared for war. Ships were taken
up, and troops embarked, but before they could arrive in
Alexandria the fighting had begun. The Egyptian army
had now entirely thrown off the authority of the khedive,
and the people in general had joined them. Their attitude became daily more threatening, and they set to
work to throw up batteries at various points on the

shore whence they could command the fleet as it lay at anchor in the harbour. Admiral Seymour, who was in command, sent orders to them to desist, but relying upon the strength of the forts they continued their work. whereupon the fleet at once prepared for action.

2. BOMBARDMENT OF ALEXANDRIA.

The French fleet refused to make common cause with us, and steamed out of the harbour. The merchant vessels and the men-of-war of other countries in the port followed their example. The European inhabitants of the city, for the most part, went on board the steamers, and when all was in readiness the British fleet steamed up and took up its position facing the outer fort of the town. At seven o'clock on the morning of the 5th of July the signal was made to commence the action, and the eight great ironclads, the *Invincible, Monarch, Penelope, Sultan, Alexandra, Superb, Inflexible* and *Temeraire*, at the same moment opened fire with their huge guns on the Egyptian forts. These also were armed with very heavy cannon, and at once replied to the fire.

The roar of the heavy guns of the fleet and batteries was tremendous. The guns were far heavier than had ever before been employed in war. To their deep booming sound was added that of the cannon of the British gunboats, the rattle of the machine-guns and of the musketry of the Egyptian troops. The Egyptian gunners stuck to their guns with the greatest bravery in spite of the tremendous fire from our ships. Fortunately their skill was by no means great, and the shot and shell from their heavy guns almost all passed over our vessels. These were, however, repeatedly struck by the missiles

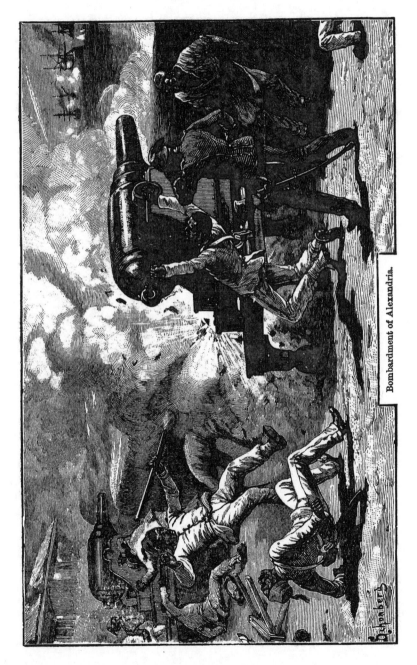

Bombardment of Alexandria.

from the smaller guns which the Egyptians were accustomed to handle.

But while comparatively little damage was being inflicted upon the British ships, our great guns were committing terrible destruction upon the forts, the explosions of the shell bringing down great masses of the masonry. Many of the Egyptian guns were soon dismounted, and great gaps made in their walls; but it was not until after four hours' tremendous fire that their guns were altogether silenced, and the enemy driven from their forts.

Several buildings lying behind the batteries had been set on fire by the bombardment, and presently volumes of smoke were seen to ascend from the European quarters of the town. Arabi's soldiers, joined by the mob, before leaving the town first plundered and then set fire to the houses inhabited by the European merchants, and an enormous destruction of property took place.

A strong body of marines and sailors were landed and took possession of the city. The progress of the flames was arrested, and after some trouble the disorder which reigned was suppressed. Many of the ringleaders of the mob were shot; some of them were caught in the very act of setting fire to houses.

3. THE ADVANCE ON CAIRO.

Meantime the troops that had been despatched both from England and India began to arrive, Sir Garnet Wolseley being in chief command. On the 19th of August, leaving one division of the army under Sir Evelyn Wood to defend the town, Sir Garnet embarked the rest of the troops on board the transports and proceeded to Port Said, at the mouth of the Suez Canal.

He then proceeded up the Canal to Ismailia, which was occupied without resistance. The work of landing the troops and stores at once commenced. It was not for a week later that any advance was made. Then, following the line of the canal, a small force moved out, and seven miles away the enemy were found in force.

An artillery fire was kept up all day. At night some more troops came out from Ismailia, and in the morning the advance was continued. The Egyptians fell back for some distance, and then made a stand at a spot where they had thrown up works. Our cavalry, under General Drury Lowe, pushed round so as to menace their retreat, and the Egyptians fled, great numbers of them going off in trains. Seven guns and seventy-five railway waggons loaded with provisions fell into our hands. On the 29th of August 13,000 of the Egyptians moved out from their lines with the intention of crushing the small bodies of English troops holding the advanced posts.

The garrison of Kassassin, the first to be attacked, consisted only of a battalion of marine artillery and two line regiments. In spite of the overwhelming numbers of the enemy, these defended themselves with great resolution. The Egyptian artillery had taken up positions which commanded the camp, and poured in a very heavy fire, and the Egyptian infantry advanced steadily in spite of the fire of our men. But just at this moment the British cavalry came up, consisting of the Horse and Life Guards and the 7th Dragoon Guards, with the horse-artillery, who had been stationed at a post four miles in the rear. General Lowe, as before, moved round so as to fall upon the enemy's rear.

The sun had set some time, but by the light of the

moon the enemy saw the black mass advancing across the sandy plain, and at once opened fire with a battery of artillery. Our guns replied, and the order was then given to the cavalry to charge; they rode right at the enemy's battery. In their haste the Egyptian gunners fired high, and few of our men were hit. With a tremendous cheer the British horsemen dashed at the guns. In a moment the Egyptian artillery-men were cut down, and the cavalry then rode forward and threw themselves upon the infantry drawn up in rear of the guns and speedily routed them.

The sound of artillery in their rear had at once checked the advance of the Egyptian infantry against Kassassin. The cavalry charge now threw them into utter confusion, and the plain was soon covered with flying Egyptians making their way back to their intrenched camp at Tel-el-Kebir.

4. THE BATTLE OF TEL-EL-KEBIR.

On the 9th of September the enemy again attacked in great numbers, and opened fire with thirty guns upon our camp; but we had now five regiments at Kassassin and the cavalry were also stationed there, and after some hard fighting the enemy were again defeated. Three days later the whole British army, 14,000 strong, were gathered at Kassassin. In the evening the troops moved out of camp and lay down on the ground until one o'clock; then the word was passed along quietly, the men re-formed their ranks and moved forward.

So noiseless was the march that they arrived in the darkness within 300 yards of the enemy's intrenchments at Tel-el-Kebir before they were perceived. The Highland

Brigade were advancing against the face of the camp nearest to us, and were consequently the first engaged. The instant the alarm was given a heavy fire was opened upon them. Not a shot was fired in return, but with a tremendous cheer the Highlanders dashed forward. So rapid was their attack that the Egyptians could at first make no effectual resistance, and the outer line of the intrenchments was carried with little loss.

Scarcely, however, had the Highlanders gained the crest, when the Egyptians opened a terrible fire from an intrenchment further back. The Highlanders replied to the fire for a minute or two and then again dashed forward. The Egyptians fought bravely, and for a short time the struggle was severe. Then some of the Highlanders made their way through some openings in the intrenchments and opened a flank fire upon the Egyptians, who at once broke and fled. In the meantime the rest of the troops had attacked the camp further on. The Egyptians, warned by the firing, were on the alert, and for a time kept up a steady fire on our troops, but the news soon came that the Highlanders were already in their camp, and, seized with a panic, the whole Egyptian army fled.

The cavalry at once pushed on in pursuit. All resistance had ended, and, riding with scarce a halt, the force arrived in twenty-four hours in Cairo. There was a strong garrison here, but, terror-struck at the rout of the army at Tel-el-Kebir, they at once surrendered, and Arabi gave himself up as a prisoner. As soon as the news reached the Egyptian troops before Alexandria they also disbanded and made for their homes, and the war terminated without another shot being fired.

Chapter XXVII.—THE WAR IN THE SOUDAN.

1. HICKS PASHA'S FORCE DESTROYED.

After the battle of Tel-el-Kebir the British became
virtually masters of Egypt. The population as a whole
were by no means sorry at the change of masters, and no
attempt at insurrection took place. But another danger
was threatening Egypt. The great region known as the
Soudan, on the Upper Nile, had been conquered by Egypt,
and was still governed by Egyptian officials. Here a man
claiming to be the Mahdi, or promised Mahommedan pro-
phet, had risen, and proclaimed that he was to do wonderful deeds. He had been joined by many of the wild tribes,
and was overcoming the resistance of the Egyptian troops
in that region.

An English officer named Hicks Pasha, a general in
the Egyptian service, was in command of the Egyptian
army in the Soudan, and he was ordered to march to the
relief of El-Obeid, an important town threatened by the
Mahdi.

He asked that one British regiment at least should be
sent up to assist him, but the request was refused, and
Hicks Pasha, with a conviction that he was going to his
death, set out with his troops. When within a few miles
of El-Obeid he was attacked by the followers of the
Mahdi. The Egyptians fought stoutly, and for three
days defended themselves successfully. At the end of
that time, worn out by thirst and fatigue, they could no
longer resist; the enemy burst in upon them, and Hicks
Pasha, the officers with him, and the whole of his men
were slain (3d–5th November, 1883).

2. GENERAL GORDON.

When the news reached England it caused great sensation, and after much deliberation government determined to send out General Gordon, one of the most remarkable men of the day, to the Soudan. General Gordon's life had been full of adventure. He was a captain in the British army when, soon after the close of our war with the Chinese, the very existence of the Chinese empire was menaced by a formidable rebellion known as the Taeping rebellion. The Chinese, who had just had proofs of the advantage that discipline and training gave to European soldiers, requested that a British officer might be allowed to train their troops, and Captain Gordon was selected for the post.

No sooner did he assume the command than he effected wonders. Although he had neither time nor means to introduce anything like European discipline among the Chinese troops, he established something like order among them, and so completely gained their confidence that they were ready to follow him anywhere. Town after town was taken from the Taepings, and such heavy blows were inflicted upon them that the power of the rebellion was speedily broken. When the insurrection was at an end the Chinese government offered to bestow large rewards upon the officer who had saved the country from destruction, but he declined to accept them, and there being no further occasion for his services he returned to the British army.

The great success which Gordon had attained with the Chinese caused him to be selected by the Khedive Ismail Pasha for another appointment for which very high qualities were necessary. Among these were courage, self-reliance, and, above all, the power of managing men and of completely winning their good-will and confidence. This post was the governorship of the Soudan, including the command of the Egyptian troops there.

Here Gordon had a success as marked and brilliant as that which he had achieved in China. He completely restored order there, suppressed, to a great extent, the horrors of the slave-trade, and won an almost superstitious respect and regard not only from the Egyptian troops but from the wild tribesmen of the Soudan.

His unwearied activity, his energy, the kindness of his manner, the patience and impartiality with which he heard all complaints and rendered justice to all, the simplicity of his life, and the single-mindedness with which he devoted himself to his work, astonished and attracted the natives. The true secret of Gordon's power over those with whom he came in contact was that he never thought of himself. He was a deeply religious man, and his whole thoughts and actions were directed to doing what he believed pleasing to God. Content with the Divine approval, he cared nothing for that of man. He regarded all the work which came to his hand as God's work, and did it with all his might, deeming his own life, his own comfort and well-doing, as considerations of no importance.

He had left the Soudan some years, and was upon the point of going out to Africa for an association of which the King of Belgium is at the head, when he received the request of government to go out again to the Soudan to arrange matters there. He started a few days later on his arduous enterprise.

General Gordon releasing Prisoners.

3. DEFEAT OF GENERAL BAKER'S ARMY.

But while General Gordon was travelling towards the Soudan other incidents of an exciting nature were taking place. One of the lieutenants of the Mahdi, named Osman Digna, had roused the tribes on the western shores of the Red Sea, was threatening the port of Suakim, and had besieged the Egyptian garrisons in the towns of Sinkat and Tokar. Admiral Hewitt, who was in command of British war-vessels in the Red Sea, was ordered to protect Suakim, and anchored off the town with four sloops and gun-boats. Osman Digna and his tribesmen several times approached the town with the intention of attacking it, but the marines and sailors were landed from the ships, and the guns of the vessels threw shell over the town among the tribesmen, and each time they fell back without making any serious attack.

Thus Suakim was defended until Baker Pasha, who was in command of a newly-raised Egyptian force, came down with several thousand men. They had but little idea of discipline or of drill, and could not be depended upon to withstand the attacks of the Arab tribesmen, who had already shown what formidable foes they were by annihilating an Egyptian force of some 1500 men which had marched out from Suakim against them. There were numbers of British regiments in Egypt doing nothing, but not one of these was sent down, and Baker Pasha was left to carry out the dangerous duty of relieving the starving garrisons of Sinkat and Tokar with troops who were little better than an armed rabble.

General Baker and the British officers with him were perfectly aware of the danger of the expedition, but they determined to do their best. The force was taken down the coast by ship to Trinkitat, the port nearest Tokar. The troops landed and marched towards that town, but on the way they were attacked by the tribesmen of Osman Digna. The undisciplined troops of Baker broke directly they were attacked. Their British officers fought gallantly, but many of them were killed, the rest cut their way through the enemy and succeeded in reaching Trinkitat. The greater portion of the Egyptians were massacred almost without resistance, the rest fled to Trinkitat hotly pursued by the enemy (4th Feb. 1884).

Fortunately the latter were afraid to come within range of the guns of the ships of war and ceased their pursuit, and the survivors of Baker's force were able to get on board a ship in safety. The immediate consequence of this defeat was that the garrison of Sinkat, who had held out heroically, finding themselves without a hope of relief and without a day's provisions remaining, marched out in a body and tried to cut their way down to the port. They were, however, attacked by the hordes of the enemy and were absolutely exterminated, not one man surviving to tell the tale. The news of these events excited a burst of indignation in England, and the government determined to take the step which, had it been taken a few weeks earlier, would have saved thousands of lives. Then two or three British regiments would have been sufficient, now it was necessary, at a great cost, to send a little army to do the work.

4. DEFEATS OF THE ARABS.

The force, which was under General Graham, assembled at Suakim, and towards the end of February landed at

Trinkitat.   The column consisted of about 7000 men, of
whom 750 were cavalry.   The troops advanced in a
hollow square; two squadrons of cavalry scouted ahead,
the rest of the cavalry remained in readiness in the rear
of the square.   The soldiers and sailors were in high
spirits, and longing to meet the foe and avenge the
massacre of Baker's troops.

The march began early, and the enemy's scouts fell
back as the cavalry advanced.   Their main position was
soon made out.   It was close to the wells of El Teb, and
a number of flags could be seen floating in the air on the
crest of a ridge about a mile in length.   As the column
approached the ridge it was seen to be swarming with
men, and guns were planted at various points.   The
position was a strong one.   Were it attacked in front
the troops would have been mown down by the artillery
and musketry fire of the enemy concealed among the
bushes, the general therefore determined to march along
its face round the end of the ridge, and to attack it in
rear.   As the column moved along the enemy opened
fire with musketry and cannon.   General Baker was
badly wounded in the face, and many men were struck
down, but not a shot was fired until the column had
passed round the ridge.   There the infantry lay down;
the sailors opened fire upon the enemy with the Gatlings,
and the artillery-men with eight seven-pounder guns
drawn by camels.

The enemy replied with six Krupp guns which they
had captured from Baker's force.   These were well served,
for the garrison of Tokar had three days before surrendered, and were fighting in the ranks of the rebels.
After half an hour's firing the enemy's guns were silenced,

the word was given, and the men sprang to their feet cheering, and the square marched straight to the enemy's position. As they approached the enemy's line the natives rushed fiercely down upon them, but they were swept away by the fire of the musketry and machine-guns. Only a few of the Arabs got to close quarters, and these were unable to break through the line of bayonets.

The square now moved on along the ground occupied by the enemy. From every bush, and from holes dug in the ground, parties of natives leapt up and dashed reck-lessly at the troops, fighting with a desperate courage which excited the admiration of our soldiers. But at last the whole ground occupied by them was captured, and they fell back. The cavalry out on the plain had charged a body of the enemy there, but had suffered severely, for the Arabs threw themselves on the ground, stabbed the horses as they rode over them, or, springing up, hurled their spears into the backs of the soldiers. The next day a portion of the column marched on to Tokar and brought off such of the townspeople as wished to leave; the force then re-embarked and were landed at Suakim, and marched thence to attack the force under Osman Digna at Tamanieb.

They encamped for the night a short distance from the enemy's position. A fire was maintained for hours by the enemy scattered among the bushes, but little harm was done, and the next day the advance was made in two squares. The first of these was composed of the 42d and 65th Regiments with the marines and sailors. As this square advanced the enemy swarmed down to the attack. A tremendous fire was opened upon them by the sailors, by the machine-guns, and by the muskets of the troops; but the natives in spite of their heavy losses still came on, and, breaking in at a gap between the 65th and the 42d, burst right into the square. For a time all was confusion, the troops and the natives being all mixed up together, and the troops fell back suffering heavily.

The misfortune would have been a very serious one had not the second square, under General Buller, come up in splendid order to their assistance, firing volley after volley into the masses of the enemy as they advanced. This checked their pursuit; the broken square re-formed and advanced with that of General Buller, and the natives, unable to withstand the heavy fire of the breech-loaders, broke and fled, leaving over 3000 dead behind them. This brought the campaign to an end, and the troops soon after re-embarked, a force being left as before to hold Suakim (March, 1884)

Chapter XXVIII.—THE NILE EXPEDITION.

1. THE ASCENT OF THE RIVER.

General Gordon had reached Khartoum, the capital of the Egyptian Soudan, in February, 1884. He was received with the greatest enthusiasm by the people, and immediately set about his work. He sent down word that he would retire from Khartoum if he could bring down with him the soldiers and inhabitants of the town, but this he could not do unless a road were opened to Suakim, the nearest port. He therefore begged that two cavalry regiments of Graham's force might be allowed to open the road from Suakim. The request was refused, Graham's troops were withdrawn, and Gordon was left unaided. For months he was shut up in Khartoum, which was besieged by the Mahdi's followers.

But although the government were willing to abandon General Gordon to his fate, the country was more jealous of the national honour. The excitement spread rapidly, and the most indignant protests against the desertion of the chivalrous soldier, who had gone out to the post of danger at the bidding of government, were made in the newspapers, at public meetings, and in Parliament.

At length government was compelled by the force of public feeling to despatch a force to the Soudan. Lord Wolseley (formerly Sir Garnet) was appointed in command of the expedition, and preparations were made on a large scale for the undertaking. Light iron steamers, to be carried out and put together on the Nile, were purchased; a large number of flat-bottomed boats were ordered from several boat and ship builders; and a corps of Canadian boatmen, experienced in the management of boats in dangerous rapids, was brought over.

The expedition did not set out until some months after the time that Lord Wolseley had urged should be chosen if Gordon's rescue was to be accomplished. It was a remarkable one in all ways. The river Nile is in many places broken up by cataracts and rapids which were considered even by the natives to be impassable at the time at which the expedition came along. But all difficulties were overcome by the energy, zeal, and labour of the troops. Where the river was smooth they tugged away manfully at the oars. Where cataracts were met with the boats unloaded their cargoes, and the men harnessed themselves to ropes, and, with the aid of numbers of Arabs, towed them along through the broken waters, in some places for many miles, until the cataracts were passed. Then the stores were carried up, placed in the boats, and the voyage was continued until another obstacle was met with.

2. THE ADVANCE ACROSS THE DESERT.

At last, in December, the leading regiments arrived at Korti far up the Nile. On their way they had learned that Colonel Stewart, who had been General Gordon's companion, had been sent down by the general in a steamer with some other Europeans. Coming down the river the steamer struck on a shoal. All on board landed, and were received with apparent friendship by the natives, but when engaged in conversation in the house of one of the chiefs the natives suddenly fell upon Stewart and his companions and murdered them, and afterwards slew all the crew of the steamer.

Lord Wolseley had at first intended to perform the whole of the journey by water, but learning that General Gordon's position at Khartoum was desperate, he determined to push on without delay across the desert. The river here makes an immense bend round by Berber, and by marching straight across the desert to Metemmeh, several weeks would be saved. Lord Wolseley had already made preparations for this march should it be found necessary. He had provided a kind of cavalry force in which camels took the place of horses. There was in addition a camel battery and camel field-hospital and transport companies. These had not gone up in the boats, but had marched along the river bank, and the men were now accustomed to their strange steeds, and were capable of executing many cavalry manœuvres.

The plan was that General Sir Herbert Stewart was to advance across the desert to Metemmeh, establishing fortified posts at the wells along the route. Sir Charles Wilson was then with an escort of infantry to go on board the steamers which General Gordon was to send down to Metemmeh, and to go up in them to Khartoum. If he brought down news that General Gordon was very sorely pressed General Stewart would have pushed straight forward and have fought his way to him. If the report was that he could hold on for some time longer, Lord Wolseley would have come on from Korti with more troops, and a general advance would have been made.

3. THE BATTLE OF ABU-KLEA.

At the same time that General Stewart's column was to cross the desert a force was to continue the ascent of the river in boats to punish the murderers of Colonel Stewart, to clear out the rebels from Berber, and to join General Stewart's force at Metemmeh should it still be there when they arrived. The small body of cavalry— five troops in all—with the expedition was divided between the two columns.

The desert march was a singular one. The camel corps had first gone up half-way to clear out the wells and to establish depots of provisions at them. This was done as far as Gakdul without opposition, and the column, marching at night and resting in the day, arrived there in three marches. They then continued their journey in a body, leaving a guard at each of the wells. They were approaching the wells at Abu-Klea when a great body of the enemy, who had marched out, some from

Metemmeh, some from Berber, advanced against them (17th January, 1885). The camel guns opened fire upon the enemy, but did not check their advance. The troops rapidly fell into the order of battle previously arranged. The camels were all made to kneel down, and around them the troops formed in a hollow square.

The Arabs came on with magnificent bravery, in spite of the heavy fire which was poured into them, and hurled themselves upon one of the faces of the square. For a moment the British line was driven back in spite of the efforts of its officers. Among these was Colonel Burnaby, an officer of extreme bravery and great personal strength. He had performed several adventurous journeys, had fought by the side of General Baker in the disastrous fight near Suakim, and was one of the most popular men in the army.

Stepping out in front of his men he tried to stem the torrent of the Arabs, but with several of the officers was killed. The men, falling back upon the camels, soon rallied. Their comrades on the other sides of the square poured their fire into the Arabs. The leading ranks of the enemy were shot down and the rest took to flight, leaving great numbers of the dead scattered all round the square. The exhausted soldiers, who were suffering greatly from thirst, now pressed forward to the wells, round which the enemy had been so lately encamped, and after a few hours' rest prepared to resume their journey.

4. TOO LATE.

It was not intended to march straight upon Metemmeh, which had been strongly intrenched by the enemy, but to strike the river a few miles above that town. All night the column marched through the desert.   The men were exhausted by the continued night marches and by want of sleep, for it was difficult to get any sleep under the burning rays of the sun in the daytime, and in the morning they halted for a short rest.   The river was now about three or four miles away, but many of the camels had broken down and it was absolutely necessary to stop for a time.   Scarcely had the troops halted when the enemy were seen approaching, and in a short time a scattering fire of musketry was opened (18th January).

The enemy were in great numbers, and it was evident that, encumbered by the baggage and animals, the column would have great difficulty in fighting its way through the crowd of enemies.   Accordingly, an intrenchment was formed with the stores and saddles; and the camels were left here under a guard commanded by Lord Charles Beresford.   The main body then proceeded on their march towards the river with the intention of fighting their way there, intrenching themselves on its bank, and then coming out to bring in the camels and baggage.

The enemy soon rushed down to the attack, but this time the troops were thoroughly prepared for them, and not a shot was thrown away until they were comparatively close.   Then such a tremendous fire was opened that they soon came to a halt, and without pushing their attack home they turned and fled back to Metemmeh.

Although the number of men lost in this battle was comparatively small, the consequences were serious, for General Stewart received a wound from which he died a few days afterwards.   The loss of the general caused a most unfortunate delay.   Colonel Burnaby had been named by Lord Wolseley to take the command in case anything happened to Sir Herbert Stewart; but he too had been killed, as we have seen. The command now fell upon Sir Charles Wilson, who, instead of embarking at once in the steamers which General Gordon had just sent down, remained two or three days trying to learn if the enemy were advancing in force, and arranging various details. Then he started up the river.

When Sir Charles Wilson approached Khartoum, a heavy fire was poured into the steamers, but no guns of welcome sounded from the walls, no British flag was flying above the governor's house. He had arrived too late; two days earlier and he would have been in time, but the delay had been fatal. A treacherous officer had opened one of the gates, the enemy had rushed in, had killed General Gordon, and captured the town. As the steamers returned with the sad news they were fired upon and so injured that those on board had to leave them and disembark on an island.

When the news reached the British camp Lord Charles Beresford at once set out in a steamer. He fought his way past a battery, and met Sir Charles Wilson with his men marching down the opposite bank, which was fortunately free of the enemy. The party were taken on board. On the return voyage the battery again opened fire, and one of the shot penetrated the boiler and so disabled the engine. The boat was anchored, and while her guns and the musketry fire from the soldiers kept down the fire of the battery, the engineers managed to patch up the boiler, and the steamer proceeded safely down to Metemmeh (9th February).

At first the troops could hardly believe that the hero they had struggled so far and fought so hard to rescue had been killed when help was almost in sight, but the sad news was verified by various native messengers, and the column pre-pared to return to Korti.

In the mean-time the column proceeding up the river had had its share of fighting, but its advance was stopped when orders had been received from home that Lord Wolseley was to retire with his army. The troops on the Nile were then withdrawn.

Lord Wolseley.

The soldiers who laid General Stewart in his lonely grave in the desert must surely have thought of the lines on the burial of Sir John Moore.

THE BURIAL OF SIR JOHN MOORE.

Not a drum was heard—not a funeral note,
    As his corpse to the ramparts we hurried;
Not a soldier discharged his farewell shot
    O'er the grave where our hero we buried.

We buried him darkly, at dead of night,
    The sods with our bayonets turning;

P

By the struggling moon-beam's misty light,
  And the lantern dimly burning.

No useless coffin inclosed his breast;
  Not in sheet or in shroud we wound him;
But he lay—like a warrior taking his rest,
  With his martial cloak around him.

Few and short were the prayers we said,
  And we spoke not a word of sorrow:
But we steadfastly gazed on the face of the dead,
  And we bitterly thought of the morrow!

We thought, as we hollowed his narrow bed,
  And smoothed down his lonely pillow,
That the foe and the stranger would tread o'er his head,
  And we far away on the billow.

Lightly they'll talk of the spirit that's gone,
  And o'er his cold ashes upbraid him;
But little he'll reck, if they let him sleep on
  In the grave where a Briton has laid him!

But half of our heavy task was done,
  When the bell tolled the hour for retiring;
And we heard the distant and random gun
  That the foe was sullenly firing.

Slowly and sadly we laid him down,
  From the field of his fame fresh and gory;
We carved not a line, and we raised not a stone,
  But we left him alone, with his glory!—*Wolfe.*

5. FIGHTING AT SUAKIM.

Osman Digna had very soon rallied after his two
defeats by General Graham's force, and another expedi-

tion was prepared and sent to Suakim. It was remarkable because not only were native regiments brought from India, but the Australian colonists sent troops to fight side by side with those of the mother country. Two battles were fought. In the first of these a column marched out to some wells occupied by the enemy. They were attacked in great force, but defeated the enemy with slaughter. On their return march they were harassed by the Arabs, but returned to camp without suffering heavy loss. The other engagement was of a more serious character.

General Sir John M'Neil was sent out with a column to form an intrenchment, or as it was called *zareba*, half-way to Tamanieb, where Osman Digna's force was assembled. Sir John M'Neil had with him the Berkshire Regiment, a naval brigade, and two Indian regiments. There was no water there, and the column took with it an immense number of camels and mules carrying water and provisions. The spot selected for the halting-place was covered with bushes, and these the soldiers began at once to cut down to form three inclosures—a large one for the stores, animals, and Indian troops, with small ones at two of the corners to be held by the Berkshire Regiment and the Naval Brigade.

A portion of the men were kept under arms, while the rest were employed in cutting the bushes and making the intrenchments. Before the work was completed the natives, who from the distant hills had seen the column moving across the plain, crept up through the bushes, many thousand strong. The few cavalry scouts of the column were out among the bushes, and they had barely time to dash in with the news that the enemy was at hand when the Arabs burst out. For a time a terrible scene of confusion took place. The animals, panic-stricken at the yells and fierce rush of the enemy, dashed through the large unfinished inclosure, pursued by the Arabs stabbing them with their long spears and knives.

The Indian regiments were for a time broken by the rush; the animals with their drivers fled towards Suakim, pursued by a portion of the natives, who killed numbers of men and beasts. The Indian troops soon rallied and opposed a stout front to their foes. The Berkshire men and the corps of marines and sailors defended their respective inclosures, stoutly repulsing every attack of their swarming foes, and aiding the Indian regiments by pouring sweeping volleys among their assailants.

The Arabs fought with the most reckless bravery, but they were unable to withstand the terrific fire of the breech-loaders, and at last fell back after suffering terrible loss. After this defeat their power of resistance was gone, and when the whole force marched out against Tamanieb the Arabs retired into the hills, and their village was burned without resistance. The heat had by this time become so great that it was all but insupportable for the Europeans, and the expedition re-embarked in ships. Some of the Indian regiments remained a considerable time at Suakim in case Osman Digna should again take the offensive, and although he and his tribesmen cannot stand against the power of the British arms, they still continue to give trouble at Suakim. Egypt still remains under the protection of England.

Chapter XXIX.—THE QUEEN AND HER SUBJECTS.

1. THE JUBILEE OF 1887.

During the years that have elapsed since 1884 no public events at home have excited such wide-spread enthusiasm and interest as the celebration of the fiftieth year of the Queen's reign in 1887, and the similar but even more remarkable occurrence, the sixtieth year of her reign ten years later. The first of these was called the Jubilee, while the second was popularly known as the Diamond Jubilee.

The first was celebrated with an enthusiasm without parallel to that time, and the people of India and the Colonies joined with those of the United Kingdom in manifestations of loyalty and affection for their sovereign. In every town there were festivals, decorations, and illuminations. Great bonfires blazed on the top of some 200 of the highest hills in England, Scotland, and Wales.

In London the occasion was observed with extraordinary pomp and ceremony. Every court in Europe sent members of its royal family, the Kings of Denmark, Saxony, and Greece being personally present, while several of the great princes of India came over to pay the Queen their homage. From end to end London was gaily decorated with flags, banners, and loyal inscriptions, and an enormous crowd assembled to witness the passage of the Queen, her family, and royal guests to Westminster Abbey, where a solemn thanksgiving service was held. At night the whole city was illuminated.

Her Majesty the Queen.

From a photograph by Messrs. Bassano, London.

Many other splendid fêtes took place in honour of the occasion: a great review of the troops was held by the Queen at Aldershot and one of the navy at Spithead. In London, and in many towns throughout the country, feasts were given to vast numbers of school children, and it may be said that all classes participated in the rejoicing.

2. THE DIAMOND JUBILEE, 1897.

But great as was the enthusiasm on that occasion, it was far surpassed by that excited by the celebration of the sixtieth anniversary of her reign. On this occasion St. Paul's Cathedral was selected as the central point of the celebration. Every house, every window along the line that would be traversed by the royal procession, was let at a very high price. Hundreds of thousands of people from all parts of the country came up to witness an event unparalleled in our history.

Contingents of native troops from India, and from all our colonies, came to represent their peoples. Not only the various colonies of Australia, New Zealand, and Canada sent mounted troops, but the West Indian Islands, Hong Kong, and our possessions on the West Coast of Africa were represented. Many of the crowned heads of Europe would have been present, but it was thought that the fatigue that would be entailed upon the Queen by the entertainment of such guests had best be avoided.

The procession, which included the ambassadors of all Continental nations, comprised squadrons from all the cavalry regiments at home and a large force of horse and foot artillery, together with sailors and marines. The streets were lined along the whole length of the route by British infantry, regulars, and volunteers. Every house was decorated from roof to basement, and stages and balconies were erected in front of many of them, while every unoccupied piece cf ground contained stands holding thousands of persons.

The Queen went to St. Paul's by Piccadilly, the Strand, and Ludgate Hill, and was greeted, as she passed along, with frantic enthusiasm. At the steps she was received by the ecclesiastical and civil dignitaries of the nation. Anxious that the poorer portions of the population should have their share in the festival, the Queen crossed to the Surrey side of the river, and after making a wide circuit recrossed at Westminster Bridge, and returned to Buckingham Palace by way of the Mall.

Throughout the country the occasion was observed with as much enthusiasm as that displayed in the capital. Fêtes were organized for the poor; while for the children of the schools there were decorations, fêtes, and fireworks. So great and general an outburst of loyalty has never been witnessed in any country, and the feeling that the Queen is not only the sovereign of her people, but their mother, was universal.

3. THE QUEEN AND HER PEOPLE.

As years had rolled on, the general affection for the Queen had increased and deepened. The nation had rejoiced with her on the occasions of the marriage of her children. It had mourned with her over the loss of her husband, of her daughter Princess Alice of Hesse, of her son Prince Leopold, of Prince Henry of Battenberg, the husband of Princess Beatrice, and over that of the Emperor Frederick, husband of her eldest daughter.

While always taking the keenest interest in the happiness of her people, of late years that interest seemed to deepen, as was shown by her enquiries on the occasion of any calamity, such as a terrible wreck, a great colliery explosion, or a disastrous fire attended with great loss of life. This interest was never so general and so marked as during the war in South Africa, when not only did she despatch frequent telegrams to the troops, expressing her admiration of their courage, and grief at their losses, but she sent numerous messages of sympathy to wives or parents who had lost loved ones there, and even requested that their photographs should be sent to her. Loyal as her people had been throughout her reign, deep as had been the interest in all relating to her, and real the affection with which she was regarded, those feelings were greatly intensified during the progress of the war, and it may be doubted whether any monarch of any nation has ever been so universally beloved by the people over whom he ruled.

Chapter XXX.—EGYPTIAN AFFAIRS.

1. THE CONQUEST OF THE SOUDAN AND BRITAIN'S WORK IN EGYPT.

The retirement of the army, after its failure to reach Khartoum in time to rescue General Gordon, left the Egyptian province of the Soudan at the mercy of the Mahdi and his horde of fanatics. These converted the country into a desert by the slaughter of the peaceful tribesmen, the destruction of their towns, and the wasting of their fields. Several times they attempted to carry their arms into Egypt itself. These efforts were repulsed by the native troops, raised and commanded by British officers.

Gradually this force increased in strength and discipline, until it was considered that the time had come when it could not only stem the tide of barbarism but rescue the Soudan from the terrible tyranny of the Khalifa—the Madhi's successor—and avenge the murder of General Gordon. A few years before, it had been considered that the Egyptian peasant, rendered timid and submissive by many generations of oppression and tyranny, could hardly be converted into a good fighting man, but this had been effected by the very able British officers who had in turn been in command of them, and by those who acted as their regimental officers. At this time the army was fortunate in having for its sirdar, or commander-in-chief, Sir Herbert Kitchener, an officer who for upwards of twenty years had been employed in Egypt, who possessed a perfect knowledge of its people, and exceptional powers of organization. In addition to the native troops, he had under his command a British force and the assistance of gunboats manned by British sailors.

The first season's campaign resulted in the driving back of the tribesmen beyond the town of Dongola. There was some sharp fighting before reaching that town, but the fanatics, brave as they were, were unable to stand against the superior weapons and discipline of their assailants.

In preparation for the next advance a railway was constructed across the desert. The difficulties were great, but the ardour of the troops, the willing and cheerful labour of the Egyptian soldiers, and the energy of their commander, overcame all obstacles, and the railway was constructed in a surprisingly short space of time.

The second campaign was as successful as the first had been. After defeating the force that opposed them, the troops continued their southward march, and occupied, without opposition, the important town of Berber and the country for some distance beyond it. Another period of inaction followed. The Khalifa's forces were now gathering to offer a desperate resistance to any farther advance. They committed terrible atrocities upon the peaceful tribesmen. Further reinforcements of the British troops arrived, and the advance commenced. The enemy occupied a strong position in a wood, on the river Atbara, which they had fortified with a palisade. It was attacked with great gallantry, and carried by assault, the Egyptian troops vieing with the British in bravery and conduct. The enemy fled, and no further stand was made until the army approached Omdurman, the capital of the Khalifa.

2. OMDURMAN AND KHARTOUM.

Omdurman lies a few miles from Khartoum, now little more than a heap of ruins, and it was here that the Khalifa was determined to make his last stand. His army was numerous and composed of men devoted to their leader, confident in their own prowess, and with a fixed belief in their invincibility. As they had proved in their battles on the shores of the Red Sea and with Lord Wolseley's expedition, they were recklessly brave, absolutely careless of life, and at close quarters formidable to even the best European troops.

As was their custom they poured down against the

position occupied by our troops, who were arranged in a curve, one wing being thrown forward. When at a distance of some 1200 yards a storm of musketry was opened upon them, while our artillery swept them with

Lord Kitchener.
From a photograph by Bassano.

shrapnel shell. Terrible as was the slaughter the tribesmen still pressed forward bravely, but heroism availed nothing against that terrible hail of lead and iron; they were literally mown down, and even their leaders never arrived within 200 yards of the fighting line of the Egyptians, against whom their principal effort was directed. Consequently the losses on our side were comparatively insignificant, the principal portion occurring among the cavalry, who in their pursuit came suddenly down into a deep water-course where some thousands of the tribesmen were hidden, and suffered heavily before they could cut their way through their assailants.

On the other hand, thousands of the Khalifa's followers perished, the rest scattered, but the tyrant himself, with a party of his immediate followers, escaped. The gunboats moving up the river opened a heavy shell fire upon Omdurman, and the enemy fled. They evacuated the

The Gordon Memorial Service at Khartoum.

town, which was taken possession of by our army without further fighting.   Next day Khartoum, which Gordon had so bravely defended and where he had been treacherously murdered, was occupied, and a religious service held in honour of the dead hero.

3. THE WORK OF PACIFICATION.

The work of pacification now began.   The British regiments were, with one or two exceptions, sent back to Britain, and officers appointed for the civil administration of the country.   The tomb of the Mahdi was destroyed, so that the superstition that, although dead, he would still protect his burying-place and would in time reappear to lead the tribesmen to victory, might be eradicated.   The Sirdar returned for a brief rest to England, and at the outbreak of the war in South Africa joined Lord Roberts in the capacity of chief of his staff, Sir Francis Wingate being appointed sirdar.

In the meantime the Khalifa had been joined by the scattered tribesmen and was at the head of an army almost as numerous as that which had fought at Omdurman.   By some rapid marches General Wingate came upon him and defeated him with great slaughter.   The Khalifa himself did not attempt to fly, but, sitting down, surrounded by his principal chiefs, met his death unflinchingly.   The victory was as complete as that of Omdurman, and was in one sense even more meritorious, since General Wingate had with him only a small number of British troops; and the result showed that the Egyptians, commanded by British officers, were now capable of taking their own part against the fanatics whom they had a few years before regarded as invincible.   Owing, however, to the nation's attention being wholly occupied with the serious struggle in South Africa, this great victory attracted far less attention and received much less credit from the nation than it deserved.

The work of pacification was now complete, and the people of Great Britain can view with just pride the result of their occupation of Egypt. They had found a country poor and in danger of overthrow by a horde of barbarians, the people ground down by taxation and oppressed by rapacious officials. It was now flourishing and contented. The people had been relieved of most of their burdens; the officials had been either dismissed or deprived of their power to maltreat the people; the course of justice had been purified; the products of the country largely increased; the revenues had grown until they exceeded the expenditure; an army amply sufficient for the wants of the country had been raised; the barbaric power that threatened the country had been destroyed, and a great province recovered. Even the young Khedive—who from listening to bad advice was at one time opposed to British influence—is quite reconciled to it, perceiving the enormous benefit that it conferred upon his country. He now warmly co-operates with us in our endeavours to raise the condition and improve the resources of Egypt.

Chapter XXXI.—BRITON AND BOER.

1. THE WAR IN SOUTH AFRICA.

In the year 1899 the most serious war in which Great Britain had been engaged during the Queen's reign broke out in South Africa. That important colony was largely peopled by men of Dutch and French extraction. A large number of these were scattered over Cape Colony and Natal, but the majority were gathered in the Orange Free State and the Transvaal.

The former of these districts was wholly independent and had always lived on good terms with us. The inhabitants of the latter, though nominally subject to the suzerainty of the Queen, were virtually independent. They were opposed to improvement of any kind, lived as their fathers had lived, in the roughest way, were for the most part wholly uncultured and illiterate, were too ignorant to cultivate the rich land that they held, and were content to live on the produce of their flocks and herds. They treated the native peoples within their boundaries almost as slaves, and shot or ill-treated them at their pleasure.

Previous to the Zulu War the Boers of the Transvaal were threatened with invasion by that warlike people, and their neighbours the Swazis and Basutos, and were glad to place themselves under British protection. As soon, however, as we had crushed the Zulus and forced the Basutos to abandon their predatory habits, the Boers rose in insurrection, besieged the towns occupied by British traders, and inflicted a heavy disaster upon a small body of British troops commanded by General Colley. The British Government of the day shrank from the struggle and granted the Boers' demands, thereby bringing ruin upon the British settlers in the country, and giving over the hapless natives to the Boers' cruel mercies.

Only a nominal suzerainty was retained; peace was

patched up, and might have been maintained for many
years had it not been for the discovery of rich deposits
of gold in the country. To work these, great numbers of
English miners and mechanics flocked into the Transvaal.
This acted prejudicially in two ways. The Boers beheld
with jealousy the increas-
ing numbers of Europeans
among them, and by
heavy taxation obtained
great sums of money,
which enabled them to
begin preparations on a
great scale for a war
with this country. They
formed an alliance with
the Orange Free State
and entered into a com-
munication with the
Dutch farmers scattered
throughout Cape Colony
and Natal.

Right Hon. Joseph Chamberlain, M.P.,
Secretary of State for the Colonies.

From a photograph by Elliott & Fry, London.

In view of the easy vic-
tories they had gained at
Laing's Nek and Majuba Hill, they believed that they
could drive the British altogether out of South Africa
and create a great Boer republic there. With this intent
they proceeded to build forts, to import great quantities
of cannon, muskets, and ammunition. In spite of the
fact that the British population equalled in numbers that
of the Boers in the Transvaal, possessed all the intelligence and enterprise, and paid practically all the taxes
of the state, they were denied any voice in its govern-

ment. They were treated rather as if they were a conquered people than free men, and were constantly insulted and ill-used.

The corruption of the governing Boers was open and unbridled, and the President, the members of his family, and the leading officials gained enormous wealth by these means. The evil became so serious a one that the British Colonial Secretary, Mr. Chamberlain, was forced to remonstrate seriously and to demand that a certain amount of representation should be granted to the European colonists there. For months Mr. Kruger, the President of the Transvaal, parleyed and quibbled, but when all was ready for war he sud-

General White.
From a photograph by Langfier, Limited.

denly sent in an insolent ultimatum, and two days later his forces and those of the Free State invaded Natal on the East, and on the other side besieged Kimberley and Mafeking.

2. THE PROGRESS OF THE WAR.

Up to this time the British had but a few thousand troops in South Africa, and had abstained from sending out an army because this would have given the Boers the opportunity of declaring that, while pretending to negotiate, war had been determined upon; consequently at first the Boers had it all their own way. In Natal they compelled the force of some 4000 men under General Symons, that had advanced to Dundee and had at first inflicted a check upon them, to retire to Ladysmith, its general having lost his life in the battle. The force at that town under General White inflicted a heavy blow on the Boers at Elandslaagte, but were then obliged to fall back in view of the immense force gathering round them. The Boers broke up the railway line to Pietermaritzburg and established a siege.

General Buller.

From a photograph by C. Knight.

In the meantime large forces were on their way out. Some 5000 troops from India had been the first to arrive, and these were with General White in Ladysmith. The Boers had reckoned upon seizing this town without difficulty, as it was situated in a valley surrounded by hills and was wholly unfortified. They soon discovered their mistake, and the defence of the town for six weeks enabled some 20,000 men to arrive and to march to its relief under General Buller.

Another force had landed at Cape Town under the

command of Lord Methuen, and advanced to the relief of Kimberley. In Cape Colony itself a large number of the Boer farmers had risen and were plundering and ill-treating their loyalist neighbours, and it is certain that, but for the arrival of the troops, the whole of the Dutch population in South Africa would have risen.

General Buller's task was one of great difficulty. Between Ladysmith and Estcourt, where his army assembled, ran the Tugela, a wide and deep river. Beyond this was a mountainous region. On the hills were planted cannon of the newest construction, obtained from Germany and France, and large numbers of machine-guns, while the slopes were cut up with deep trenches in which the Boers could lie secure from our fire while able to mow down the troops advancing to the attack. On the British side none doubted that they would without great difficulty overcome the Boer defence, occupied only by men untrained in warfare, although individually good shots. The attack was delivered on December 15th at three points, but although the British soldiers fought with heroic bravery they failed to obtain any advantage and were obliged to fall back with heavy losses and to wait until reinforcements came up.

Not until January 16th was General Buller in a position to make another attack, his force having now increased to 30,000 men. This time the Tugela was crossed, and for nearly a week the troops, aided by their powerful artillery, endeavoured to break through the Boer position, but in vain, and after serious loss withdrew across the river. The Boer artillery was equally strong, and, with the exception of the naval guns, was greatly superior to our own. An almost impregnable

Dundonald entering Ladysmith.

mountain in Spion Kop was taken by surprise, but the
fire opened upon it was so terrible that its capturers
were forced on the following day to retire.

On February 5th the attack was renewed, more guns
had been got up on the heights, the river was crossed
without resistance, the Boers were driven back and a
position which it was believed would open the way to
Ladysmith was captured at the point of the bayonet.
Beyond this, however, it was impossible to advance, the
hill being commanded by others in the neighbourhood.
The Boers several times tried to retake the hill, but
were driven back.   At last, after holding the position
for two days, the army again retired across the Tugela.

All this time communication had been kept open, by
means of signals, with Ladysmith, and it was known
that the situation was most serious there.   The provisions were all but exhausted, the horses of the cavalry
had been eaten, and although a serious attack of the
Boers had been repulsed it was certain that the place,
which had now been besieged for more than four months,
must surrender in a few days unless the long-looked-
for aid arrived.

A week later the left of the Boer position was attacked,
and several positions of great importance captured.
Guns being placed there, the troops were enabled to
cross the Tugela after taking the town of Colenso. Step
by step the enemy were driven backwards beyond the
line of railway.   There was tremendous fighting at
Pieters Hill, which commanded the line of railway.
This was finally captured and the way opened to Ladysmith, which was relieved on the last day of February,
the succouring party arriving just in time, for the garri-

son, which was reduced by famine, was in the last stage of weakness. The Boers fled and took up so strong a position to the north that fighting ceased for a time.

3. THE CONQUEST OF THE TRANSVAAL.

On the western side of the Orange Free State, Lord Methuen's column at first obtained some successes, driving the Boers before them from several hills they had occupied. At the Modder River, within sound of the guns of Kimberley, the Boers made a determined stand, but after suffering heavy loss retreated to a very strong position some eight miles from Kimberley. Here strong lines of defence had been erected. A night attack was attempted, but the Boers were on the alert, and when the troops were within three hundred yards of their lines they suddenly opened so terrible a fire that the Highlanders suffered fearfully, and General Wauchope, who commanded them, was killed. The surprise was a complete one, for the existence of the trench in which the Boers were lying concealed was unsuspected. After the heavy loss that they had suffered, the troops fell back on their camp on the Modder.

This failure and those suffered by Buller showed the home authorities that they had miscalculated the serious nature of the struggle. Great reinforcements were sent out under Lord Roberts, with Lord Kitchener as chief of his staff. From the first, offers of assistance had been made by the Canadian and Australian colonies, and the evidence given, by the repulses in Natal and on the Modder, of the serious nature of the situation elicited a display of enthusiastic loyalty throughout the Empire.

South Africa had already furnished large bodies of volunteers, and large numbers of mounted troops were now despatched to the scene of action by Canada, New South Wales, Victoria, Queensland, West Australia, and New Zealand, all of which did magnificent service.

Lord Roberts.
From a photograph by Russell & Sons.

Lord Roberts arrived in January, and having seen that all the preparations were complete, on February 12th moved into the Free State with 45,000 men. Making a circuit he threw himself across the Boer line of communication, while General French with the cavalry, making a wide sweep round, entered Kimberley, which had repulsed all attacks made upon it. The Boers at once left their position and retired in all haste in different directions; their commander, Cronje, with about 3000 men, was overtaken and surrounded by General Roberts at Paardeberg.

The Boers entrenched themselves on the Modder River in hopes that reinforcements would come up. Some bodies of Boers did approach, but were easily defeated, and after resisting a tremendous bombardment for ten days, Cronje surrendered with all his men.

A fortnight later General Roberts entered Bloem-

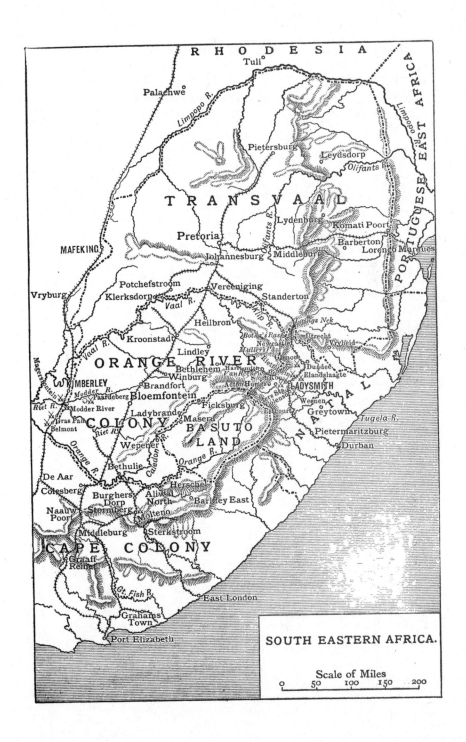

RHODESIA

Tuli

Palachwe

Limpopo R.

Pietersburg

Leydsdorp

Olifants R.

TRANSVAAL

Pretoria

Lydenburg

Komati Poort

Mafeking

Johannesburg

Middleburg

Barberton

Lorenço Marques

Vryburg

Potchefstroom

Klerksdorp

Vereeniging

Standerton

PORTUGUESE EAST AFRICA

Vaal R.

Heilbron

Laing's Nek

Potchefstroom

Kroonstad

Lindley

Botha's Pass

Mullers Pass

Utrecht

Vryheid

Newcastle

ORANGE RIVER

Bethlehem

Harrismith

Dundee

Elandslaagte

Winburg

LADYSMITH

KIMBERLEY

Paardeberg

Bloemfontein

Ficksburg

NATAL

Wegnen

Greytown

Mudder R.

Modder River

Ladybrand

Maseru

Tugela R.

Gras Pan

Belmont

Riet R.

COLONY

BASUTO

Pietermaritzburg

Riet R.

Wepener

LAND

Durban

Caledon R.

Bethulie

Orange R.

De Aar

Colesberg

Herschel

Burghers Dorp

Aliwal North

Barkley East

Naauw Poor

Stromberg

Molteno

Middleburg

Sterkstroom

CAPE COLONY

Graaff Reinet

Gt. Fish R.

East London

Grahams Town

Port Elizabeth

SOUTH EASTERN AFRICA.

Scale of Miles

0   50   100   150   200

fontein, the capital of the Orange Free State, and issued a proclamation annexing that state to the British Empire under the name of the Orange River Colony. At a later date the Transvaal was also proclaimed a British Colony.

After some time spent in making arrangements, Lord Roberts moved north with great rapidity. The Boers were now thoroughly disheartened, and offered but a feeble resistance, and the victorious troops entered first Johannesburg and then Pretoria, the capital of the Transvaal. Mafeking, which had maintained an heroic resistance under the command of Colonel Baden-Powell, was, to the delight of Britons throughout the Empire, relieved by a mixed force of British and Colonials.

Chapter XXXII.—THE FAR EAST.

1. INDIA.

In India two border wars of more than usual importance took place. The aggressive conduct of the tribes in the mountainous region to the north necessitated an expedition to Chitral. It was admirably conducted and crowned with complete success. The results were important inasmuch as it extended our power towards the crest of the mountain range and gave us the command of one of the routes by which a hostile army from the north might invade India.

The second war was of a more serious character. The warlike tribes dwelling among the almost inaccessible mountains to the west of the Khyber Pass combined in a rising against us. They had always considered that it was impossible for British troops to penetrate the passes through which alone access could be obtained to their valleys. It required a large force and an enormous transport train to carry out the necessary operations. The army was broken into columns, and these fought their way by various routes across lofty mountains and through rugged defiles. The tribesmen fought with great bravery, and our losses were heavy, but finally complete success attended the operations. Their strongholds were all taken, their villages burned, and they were forced at last to sue for peace, which was granted on the condition of the payment of heavy fines. The infliction of these, the losses they had sustained, and the knowledge brought home to them that the British arms could, in case of their future misconduct, be carried into the heart of their district, is likely to ensure tranquillity for a considerable time.

2. PLAGUE.

During the last three years of the century India has suffered from two terrible scourges. The first of these was the plague which made its first appearance in Bombay. It was of the same character as that which had ravaged Europe during the Middle Ages, and was then known as the Black Death, and again in the reign of Charles II under the name of the Plague. It spread with terrible rapidity in spite of the efforts of the sanitary authorities, and carried off great numbers of persons. The difficulty of coping with it was all the greater because of the aversion of the natives for any examination of their houses. From Bombay it spread widely, and hundreds of thousands of persons perished.

Even at the end of the century the plague is by no means extirpated, Bombay still remaining the centre of the pest. Unfortunately, medical skill has failed to find any certain remedy, and throughout the number of deaths in proportion to the attacks has been terribly large. This was partly due to the fatalism of the natives, who, when attacked by disease, made little effort to struggle against it, but resigned themselves at once to death. Among the European portion of the population the mortality has been slight.

The last year of the century has been marked by the most terrible famine that has occurred since our occupation of India. In that country the success of the crops depends entirely upon the rain that falls in what is known as the Monsoon season and extending from May to the end of July. Any failure of these rains brings the cultivator face to face with ruin and starvation. There have been several famines arising from this cause during the last fifteen years. Each of these has been met, and its horrors mitigated, by the efforts of Government, which has employed large numbers of people in the smitten districts upon the work of making roads and canals, and by importing large quantities of grain from other parts of India and even from abroad. None of these famines, however, has approached the severity of that of 1899–1900, the districts involved by it being more numerous, and the failure of the crops more complete.

The distress, however, was met by great efforts by the Indian Government; over six million persons were employed upon the relief-works, but even with this assistance the sufferings of the people have been terrible, especially in the districts still ruled over by native princes. In these districts large numbers have died. Even in those parts under our direct rule the sufferings of the whole population have been terrible, for it was possible only to distribute the smallest amount of food that would keep life together.

The prospect for the future is very dark, for when the rains commenced in the middle of June the country was so baked up that the water, instead of sinking into the soil, ran off rapidly. Moreover, the draught cattle used in cultivation have died off, the grain put aside for sowing has been consumed, and it is already evident that the resources of the Indian Government will be taxed to the utmost for some time to come before the famine districts can recover the terrible blow that has been inflicted upon them.

3. CHINA.

In China events have, during the last few years, moved rapidly. The long stagnation was broken by the outbreak of a war between that empire and the island kingdom of Japan. The latter had embraced European civilization and ways with extraordinary energy, while China had made but little effort to keep abreast of the times. The result was that she suffered a crushing defeat at the hands of a power she had previously despised.

The influence of Europe alone preserved China from disruption. Russia, ever on the watch to obtain advantages, seized Port Arthur and a large strip of territory; and Great Britain, in order to safeguard her interests, obtained a cession of Wei-Hai-Wei. So matters might

The Principal Street in Pekin.

Photo. N. P. Edwards.

have remained without further change had it not been that the Queen-mother of China, an ambitious and utterly unscrupulous woman, seized and dethroned the young Emperor, and set up a puppet prince in his place. This action excited a strong feeling of reprobation even in China itself, and she was obliged to defer the final execution of this plan, still holding the young Emperor a close prisoner in her hands.

So openly was she opposed to foreigners that a secret society, calling itself the Boxers, rose with the avowed intention of expelling all Europeans. They were favoured by the Empress, who administered strong reproofs to officials who took vigorous steps to put down the rising.

The movement spread rapidly; mission stations were attacked and destroyed, and in many cases the missionaries and their wives massacred. Thousands of native converts shared the same fate. The troops joined the Boxers. They marched against Tientsin, while the churches and chapels were burnt, and the residents besieged. Bodies of seamen and marines from the men-of-war of Great Britain, Russia, Germany, and France were landed, and under the command of Admiral Seymour marched 2500 strong for Pekin, where the various legations and European establishments were threatened with destruction. A strong Chinese force was marching to relieve the troops garrisoning the Taku forts, that command the mouth of the river. An ultimatum was sent by the ships of war to the forts. These replied by opening fire, but after a sharp bombardment the sailors and troops landed and captured the forts.

Reinforcements were now arriving from Japan, Port Arthur, and Hong Kong, and another force was landed, for Tientsin was known to be in great danger of being captured, and no news had been received whatever of

Admiral Seymour's expedition. After a sharp fight Tientsin was relieved, and the force then marched to the assistance of the admiral, who was known to be surrounded and attacked on all sides. The expedition was successful, and the force was rescued and brought in. As reinforcements arrived the native town of Tientsin was attacked, and after hard fighting captured. Great preparations were then made for an advance against Pekin

The Marquis of Salisbury.
From a photograph by Russell & Sons, London.

to rescue the Europeans there, and afterwards to take such steps as might be found necessary to restore order in China, and to reopen it again to European trade and civilization. After severe fighting Pekin was relieved and the Ambassadors saved.

Chapter XXXIII.—THE DEATH OF THE QUEEN.

Never assuredly since the world was first peopled has such general sorrow been excited as by the words flashed across land and sea on January 22nd, 1901,

"The Queen is dead". There had been but short warning—three brief days, alternating between hope and fear, all insufficient to enable men to take in the fact that the noble figure which had come to be viewed as almost an integral part of British life and British greatness was about to be removed—and then came the heavy blow.

Not only among the people of these islands, and of the great colonies sprung from them, was the news felt both as a national and a personal loss, but among the many peoples who owned her sway the feeling was no less profound. The negroes of Jamaica wept when they heard of the loss of their great Queen; the Kaffir tribesmen of South Africa mourned the loss of her under whom they had found peace and protection; the traders and handicraftsmen of India closed their shops when they heard that the great, and to them mysterious, Empress, whom some of them had almost come to worship as a divinity, was dead; and the Red Indian, who had found in Canada a home where he could live free from the hostility of greedy land adventurers, was struck with grief when he heard of the death of the great White Mother.

But not to her own subjects was this feeling of deep sorrow confined; it was scarcely less genuine and sincere among our kindred across the Atlantic, while in every capital of Europe, the rulers, public bodies, and people, vied with each other in their expressions of sorrow. Even in quarters where, of late, the press had teemed with expressions of bitter hostility to this country and its ruler, the voice of faction was hushed, and the nobility of the woman, and the beneficence of the queen, were cordially and ungrudgingly acknowledged.

No such universal tribute has ever been paid, none has been so well deserved. As a Queen her influence for good was immense; she was ever a peacemaker, and desired above all things peace, but peace with honour. Nothing was done by her ministers in any important affair without every despatch being submitted to her for approval; no step was taken without receiving her sanction. She ruled as well as reigned, quietly, and unostentatiously, ever constitutionally and wisely; and her influence was not confined to the affairs of her own empire, but was continually exercised for the good of the world in general. Her great age, her unrivalled experience, her connection by marriage with so many rulers, the known wideness of her views, her common-sense and wisdom, necessarily gave her an influence far beyond that of any other reigning monarch, and was always employed for good; and in this sense it will be long indeed before the blank, caused by her death, can be repaired.

But while as a Queen her subjects respected and admired her, it was as a woman that deep in their hearts they loved her. Her private life was a model, free from all blame and all reproach. Her sympathies were ever with suffering, she was quick to express how deeply she felt every calamity that befell even a small portion of her subjects. Quickly following a great colliery explosion, a terrible shipwreck, a disastrous conflagration, or any other accident attended by great loss of life, would come a message from her expressing her grief at the occurrence, and her deep sympathy with those whose dear ones had been taken from them. Eager as she was for peace, when war was forced upon

her, none felt a keener interest in her troops, a deeper
sympathy in their sufferings, a higher admiration for
their bravery, than their Queen; and never was this
feeling evinced more strongly than during the last
fifteen months of her life, not only in her frequent
messages to her troops in the field, but in her many
letters of sympathy to the parents, wives, and relatives,
whose dear ones had fallen in her service.   Much as she
had been loved during her long reign, it is not too
much to say that never was she enthroned so deeply in
the hearts of her subjects as during this time of stress
and suffering.

During her long reign she had witnessed vast changes.
The area over which she reigned had been enormously
increased, its population doubled, its wealth multiplied
in an even greater proportion.   From a kingdom it had
grown into a world-wide Empire, such as the world had
never before seen.   Canada, from two comparatively
small provinces, had grown into a great Dominion;
Australasia had sprung from very small beginnings into
a great and powerful Commonwealth; India had all
come under the sway of the British Crown, and under
wise government had become one of its most attached
dependencies.   From the small colony in South Africa,
British power had spread till Britain had become para-
mount in the African continent.   The Queen lived to
see the empire in the southern portion consolidated by
the annexation of the two Republics that had forced a
war for supremacy upon us.   In Egypt our influence
had become complete, our arms having stretched far
south; and ere long British influence will stretch from
the Mediterranean to the Cape.

Most gratifying of all is the fact that in the last years of the Queen's reign, the loyalty of the Colonies has been so conspicuously shown by the assistance they rendered us in the war in South Africa. So far from there being any signs of the future disintegration of our vast Empire, it is shown that the loyalty of its component parts is far more complete and heartfelt than it was when Victoria ascended the throne more than sixty years ago.

While the two other great queens who have reigned over England, Elizabeth and Anne, have at their death seen a prospect of deep trouble arising from disputed accession by foreign princes to the throne, Queen Victoria was happy in knowing that she left behind her an heir worthy to fill her place, and enjoying a popularity second only to her own. The Prince of Wales had for many years relieved her of many of the burdens of Sovereignty. He had shown himself devoted to public business, ever ready to give up his personal ease and comfort for public duty, ever ready to aid in good works, not only by his patronage, but by his active personal attendance and supervision. He was happy in having for his consort a princess who, by her charm and amiability, had won the affection of the people.

The British nation are at bottom intensely conservative. We have had no king bearing a double name, and just as the Queen selected her second name as that by which she should be crowned, so Albert Edward, Prince of Wales, announced that he would be crowned as Edward VII, thus showing the continuance of his line of descent from some of the most famous English kings. That he will reign long and happily, is the earnest hope and prayer of the mighty Empire over which he rules.